GW00360124

Microsoft
explained

Books Available

By the same authors:

BP585	Microsoft Excel 2007 explained
BP584	Microsoft Word 2007 explained
BP583	Microsoft Office 2007 explained
BP581	Windows Vista explained
BP580	Windows Vista for Beginners
BP569	Microsoft Works 8 and Works Suite 2006 explained
BP563	Using Windows XP's accessories
BP558	Microsoft Works 8.0 & Works Suite 2005 explained
BP557	How Did I Do That ... in Windows XP
BP555	Using PDF Files
BP550	Advanced Guide to Windows XP
BP548	Easy PC Keyboard Shortcuts
BP545	Paint Shop Pro 8 explained
BP544	Microsoft Office 2003 explained
BP538	Windows XP for Beginners
BP525	Controlling Windows XP the easy way
BP514	Windows XP explained
BP513	IE 6 and Outlook Express 6 explained
BP512	Microsoft Access 2002 explained
BP511	Microsoft Excel 2002 explained
BP510	Microsoft Word 2002 explained
BP509	Microsoft Office XP explained
BP498	Using Visual Basic
BP487	Quicken 2000 UK explained
BP486	Using Linux the easy way
BP465	Lotus SmartSuite Millennium explained
BP433	Your own Web site on the Internet
BP341	MS-DOS explained
BP284	Programming in QuickBASIC
BP258	Learning to Program in C

Microsoft Excel 2007 explained

by

N. Kantaris

and

P.R.M. Oliver

Bernard Babani (publishing) Ltd
The Grampians
Shepherds Bush Road
London W6 7NF
England

www.babanibooks.com

Please Note

Although every care has been taken with the production of this book to ensure that any projects, designs, modifications and/or programs, etc., contained herewith, operate in a correct and safe manner and also that any components specified are normally available in Great Britain, the Publishers and Author(s) do not accept responsibility in any way for the failure (including fault in design) of any project, design, modification or program to work correctly or to cause damage to any equipment that it may be connected to or used in conjunction with, or in respect of any other damage or injury that may be so caused, nor do the Publishers accept responsibility in any way for the failure to obtain specified components.

Notice is also given that if equipment that is still under warranty is modified in any way or used or connected with home-built equipment then that warranty may be void.

About this Book

Microsoft Excel 2007 explained was written to help users to get to grips with the new Excel spreadsheet application which is a component part of the *Microsoft Office 2007.*

Most strikingly, Excel 2007 has a completely new interface which replaces the menus, toolbars and most of the task panes and dialogue boxes with a ribbon of buttons organised into theme tabs, a Quick Access toolbar that you can customise with commands you use the most, and just one menu.

The program incorporates several new features, as well as improvements on previous Excel capabilities. The new features include:

A new interface supporting task-orientated tabs that contain groups of commands and features, instead of the old interface where commands and features were buried in complex menus and toolbars.

Worksheets which now support over 1 million rows and over 16 thousand columns.

An unlimited number of types of formatting in the same workbook, and support for 16 million colours.

You can now format Excel tables, charts, PivotTables, shapes and diagrams using styles with themes of predefined colours, fonts, lines and fill effects.

Use of conditional formatting to allow visual annotation of data to make it easier to spot trends in your data.

The formula bar now automatically re-sizes to accommodate long, complex formulae, which prevents them from covering other data in the worksheet.

Support for structured references which allow the use of named ranges and named tables in a formula.

The provision of a Page Layout View which allows you to see how your work will look in printed format before applying the changes to your data.

Excel 2007 can either be used by itself or made to share information with other Office applications. This book first introduces Excel by itself, with sufficient detail to get you working, then discusses how to share information with Word 2007 and other Office 2007 applications.

The material in this book is presented using simple language, avoiding jargon as much as possible, but with such a subject some is inevitable, so a short glossary of terms is included, which should be used with the text of this book, where necessary.

The book was written with the non technical, non computer literate person in mind, and is structured on the 'what you need to know first, appears first' basis. No prior knowledge of this program is assumed, although more experienced users don't have to start at the beginning and go right through to the end, as the chapters have been designed to be fairly self-contained.

It is hoped that with the help of this book, you will be able to come to terms with Excel 2007 and do it in the shortest, most effective, and enjoyable way. Have fun!

About the Authors

Noel Kantaris graduated in Electrical Engineering at
Bristol University and after spending three years in the
Electronics Industry in London, took up a Tutorship in
Physics at the University of Queensland. Research
interests in Ionospheric Physics, led to the degrees of
M.E. in Electronics and Ph.D. in Physics. On return to the
UK, he took up a Post-Doctoral Research Fellowship in
Radio Physics at the University of Leicester, and then a
lecturing position in Engineering at the Camborne School
of Mines, Cornwall, (part of Exeter University), where he
was also the CSM Computing Manager. At present he is
IT Director of FFC Ltd.

Phil Oliver graduated in Mining Engineering at
Camborne School of Mines and has specialised in most
aspects of surface mining technology, with a particular
emphasis on computer related techniques. He has
worked in Guyana, Canada, several Middle Eastern and
Central Asian countries, South Africa and the United
Kingdom, on such diverse projects as: the planning and
management of bauxite, iron, gold and coal mines; rock
excavation contracting in the UK; international mining
equipment sales and international mine consulting. He
later took up a lecturing position at Camborne School of
Mines (part of Exeter University) in Surface Mining and
Management. He has now retired, to spend more time
writing, consulting, and developing Web sites.

Acknowledgements

We would like to thank friends and colleagues, for their helpful tips and suggestions which assisted us in the writing of this book.

Trademarks

HP and **LaserJet** are registered trademarks of Hewlett Packard Corporation.

Microsoft, **Windows**, **Windows XP**, **Windows Vista**, **Excel**, **Word**, **Access and PowerPoint** are either registered trademarks or trademarks of Microsoft Corporation.

PostScript is a registered trademark of Adobe Systems Incorporated.

All other brand and product names used in the book are recognised as trademarks, or registered trademarks, of their respective companies.

Contents

1

Package Overview

Microsoft Excel 2007 is part of the Office 2007 suite and is fully integrated with all the other Office 2007 applications. Excel is a powerful and versatile program which has proved its usefulness over the years, not only in the business world, but with scientific and engineering users as well.

The program's power lies in its ability to emulate everything that can be done with a pencil, paper and a calculator. Thus, it is an 'electronic spreadsheet' or simply a 'spreadsheet', a name which is also used to describe it and other similar products. The program is extremely flexible and can deal with the solution of the various applications it is programmed to manage very accurately and very fast. These can vary from budgeting and forecasting to the solution of complex scientific and engineering problems.

Excel 2007 has been designed to present the new look also found in the other Office 2007 applications, and includes several improvements over the previous version of the program. These are:

Worksheets which now support 1,048,576 rows by 16,384 columns, which is 1,500% more rows and 6,300% more columns than the previous Excel 2003!

An unlimited number of types of formatting in the same workbook, instead of the 4 thousand available in the previous version.

The number of cell references per cell is now only limited by available memory.

Memory management has been increased to 2 GB. Excel 2007 now supports dual-processors and multithreaded chip sets as well as up to 16 million colours.

The formula bar now automatically re-sizes to accommodate long, complex formulae, which prevents them from covering other data in the worksheet.

The provision of a Page Layout View which you can use to create a worksheet while keeping an eye on how it will look in printed format. You can base a new workbook on a variety of templates that are installed with Excel, or you can quickly access and download templates from the Microsoft Office Online Web site.

In addition, Excel 2007 allows the creation of 3D super-spreadsheets by using multi-page workbooks which support 3D *drill-through* formulae, and includes a long list of 'goal-seeking', 'what-if?' analysis tools and an excellent set of database capabilities.

Hardware and Software Requirements

If Microsoft Excel 2007 is already installed on your computer, you can safely skip this and the next section of this chapter.

To install and use Excel 2007, which comes as part of Microsoft Office 2007, you need an IBM-compatible PC with a processor of at least 500 MHz and 256 MB of RAM, and 2 GB of hard disc space. The minimum other requirements are:

- Microsoft Windows XP with Service Pack (SP) 2, Windows Server 2003 with SP1, or later operating system such as Windows Vista.

- A CD-ROM or DVD drive.

- 1024x768 or higher resolution monitor.

- To share data among multiple computers, the host computer must be running Windows Server 2003 with SP1, Windows XP Professional with SP2, or later.

- Microsoft Internet Explorer 6.0 or later, 32-bit browser only.

- Internet functionality requires access to the Internet.

The operating system we are using here is Windows Vista, therefore the screen dumps in this book might be slightly different from yours if you are using Windows XP instead. Don't worry, however, as what is presented in this book is valid for both operating systems.

Installing Microsoft Excel 2007

To install Excel, you'll have to install Office 2007 on your computer's hard disc, a process which is now fairly painless. Simply place the distribution CD in your CD/DVD drive and close it. The auto-start program should display the screen in Fig. 1.1, and clicking the option pointed to, will start the **Setup** program.

Fig. 1.1 The AutoPlay Screen.

If the **Setup** program doesn't start automatically, click the **Start** button, and in the ***Start Search*** box type E:\setup. In our case the CD/DVD was the E: drive; yours could be different. Clicking the **OK** button, starts the installation of Microsoft Office 2007. With both methods, **Setup** first displays a message box telling you it is extracting files and then opens the Enter your Product Key window, shown in Fig. 1.2 below.

Fig. 1.2 Entering the Product Key.

From now on you just follow the instructions given. If you don't enter the Product Key code correctly you will not be able to go further though! Clicking the **Continue** button opens the next window for you to read and accept Microsoft's licence terms.

In the next window, click **Install Now** for a default complete installation of Office 2007, or click **Customize** which gives you some choices, as shown in Fig. 1.3 on the next page.

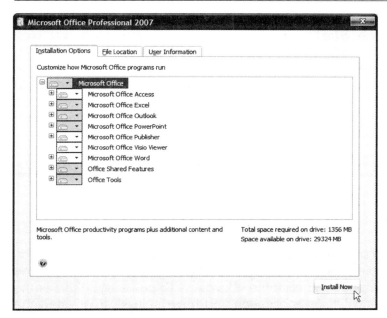

Fig. 1.3 The Installation Options Window.

The Installation Options tab, shown in Fig. 1.3, lists the Office 2007 applications to be installed and how they will run. You work your way through this list until the type of installation you want is selected. The space required and available on your hard disc is shown in the bottom right of the pane.

The File Location tab lets you set where on your hard disc(s) Office should be installed. The User Information tab lets you enter or change your name, initials and company.

Clicking the **Install Now** button, pointed to in Fig. 1.3 above, copies files to your computer's hard disc, sets up the applications and hopefully displays the window shown in Fig. 1.4 on the next page.

Fig. 1.4 The Successful Installation Window.

To start Excel 2007, use the **Start**, **All Programs** command, select the **Microsoft Office** entry from the menu, and click the **Microsoft Excel** entry. If this is the first Office application you have started, it will start the Activation Wizard, as shown in Fig. 1.5 below.

Fig. 1.5 The Office Activation Screen.

As you can see in the screen of Fig. 1.5, you have a choice as to the method of activation of Office; via the Internet, or by telephone. If you choose to activate your product through the Internet and you are not already connected, the Wizard will help you get connected.

You can launch Excel (or any of the other Office applications) for a total of 25 times before having to enter the Product Key and activating the product.

During activation, the product ID and a non-unique hardware identification are sent to Microsoft, but it does not include personal information or any data held on your computer. The product ID is generated from the product key used to install the software and a generic code representing the version and language of the Microsoft Office being activated. The non-unique hardware identification represents the configuration of your PC at the time of activation.

The hardware identification identifies only the PC and is used solely for the purpose of activation. Office can detect and accept changes to your PC configuration. Minor upgrades will not require re-activation. However, if you completely overhaul your PC, you may be required to activate your product again.

There is no software registration with the Office 2007 system. Instead, you have the option of registering for special online services from Microsoft Office Online. These include free community-submitted templates and search results tailored to the products you have installed.

The New 2007 Interface

Excel 2007 has a built-in consistency with all the other Office 2007 applications, which makes it easier to use. Previous releases of Microsoft Office applications used a system of menus, toolbars, task panes, and dialogue boxes to access commands and get things done.

Because Office 2007 applications do so much more, these features have been replaced with a new user interface which makes it easier to find and use the full range of features these new programs provide. This is somewhat daunting at first, but once you start using the new interface you will very rapidly get used to it. We will be discussing these new features in Excel in some detail in the next chapter.

In the mean time, however, let us have a quick look at Excel. To start the program use the **Start**, **All Programs** command, click the **Microsoft Office** entry, then click the **Microsoft Excel 2007** option on the drop-down sub-menu, pointed to in Fig. 1.6.

Fig. 1.6 The Microsoft Office Menu.

The opening Excel screen is displayed as shown in Fig. 1.7 on the next page. Note how different this is from previous versions of the program. The most striking difference being the presence of the **Ribbon**, which appears at the top of the worksheet replacing the previous versions' Menu bar, Formatting bar, and Toolbar.

Fig. 1.7 The Excel Opening Screen.

Note: As the width of the Excel window is made smaller the Ribbon buttons shrink to accommodate as many of them as possible on the available space.

At this point we will only have a look at the **Help** system included with Excel 2007. The rest of the opening screen will be discussed in Chapter 2.

Getting Help in Excel 2007

No matter how experienced you are, there will always be times when you need help to find out how to do something in Excel. There are several ways to get help, but don't look for the Office Assistant, as it has now been switched off for good.

The Built-in Microsoft Help System

To illustrate the built-in Help System, click the **Help** button shown here, or press the F1 function key. The Help window will open as shown in Fig. 1.8 on the next page.

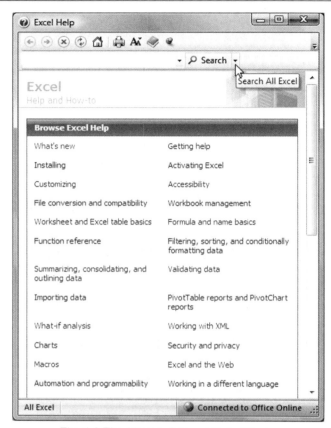

Fig. 1.8 The Microsoft Excel Help Window.

The program expects you to be 'Online'. You can control where Help searches for its content in two ways. If you click the down arrow to the right of the Search button, pointed to in Fig. 1.8 above, a drop-down menu opens as shown here in Fig. 1.9.

Fig. 1.9 The Help Options.

The Help Options drop-down menu has several online and PC based options. If you click the **Excel Help** option under **Content from this computer** the Help system will only look on your computer for its help data.

Whether you are looking at Help online or offline is shown in the lower-right corner of the Help window, as shown in Fig. 1.8 on the previous page.

Clicking this area with the mouse opens the

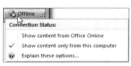

Fig. 1.10 The Help Options.

Connection Status menu shown in Fig. 1.10. As can be seen, this offers an easier way to tell Help where to look for its content. This setting is retained after you close the Help window, so if you don't want to search online you only have to set this once whatever Office application you are working with.

The Help Toolbar

At the top of the Help window (see Fig. 1.8) there are icons to help you with navigation, printing a Help topic or displaying the Table of Contents list, to mention but a few. You can control the Help window with these buttons, as follows:

Back – Opens the last Help page viewed in the current session list.

Forward – Opens the previous Help page viewed in the current session list.

Stop – Stops loading a document.

Refresh – Reloads the current Help page.

Home – Opens the first (or Home) Help page for the open application.

Print – Opens the Print dialogue box to let you print all, or a selection, of the current Help topic.

Change Font Size – Opens a sub-menu to let you control the size of text in the Help window.

Hide/Show Table of Contents – A toggle key which closes or reopens the left pane of the Help window, giving more room for the Help text.

Keep On Top/Not On Top – A toggle key you can click to keep the Help window displaying on top of, or below, any open Excel window.

Clicking the **Show Table of Contents** icon, displays an enlarged window, as shown in Fig. 1.11.

Fig. 1.11 The Microsoft Excel Help Window with Table of Contents.

The Table of Contents opens up a list of available help topics in the form of closed books . Left-clicking one of these books opens it and displays a further list of topics with an icon, as shown in Fig. 1.12.

Fig. 1.12 Using Excel Help.

Clicking any of these opens the relevant Help page in the right-hand pane as shown in Fig 1.12. We suggest you try looking up 'What's new' in Excel 2007 – it is an excellent starting point in learning how to use the **Help** System.

Searching Help

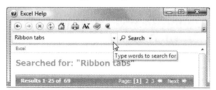

Fig. 1.13 Typing Words to Search for.

A quick way to find what you want in the Help system is to enter the text you want to search for in the **Type words to search for** box, as shown here in Fig. 1.13. A search using 2 to 7 words returns the most accurate results. If you want to repeat a search, you click the down-arrow, pointed to, to the right of the **Type words to search for** list, and then click the search term that you want in the displayed list.

The Excel 2007 **Help** system is quite comprehensive and it is usually easy to find the information you are looking for. We strongly recommend that you spend some time here. An hour now may well save many hours later!

Screen Tips

If you want to know what a particular button or feature does in Excel 2007, hover the mouse pointer over the button or feature to get **Screen Tips** help. A floating box

will appear as shown in Fig. 1.14.

Here we hovered the pointer over the **Format** Painter button and a quite detailed description was given. This feature is much improved in Excel 2007.

Fig. 1.14 A Typical Screen Tip Floating Box.

2

The Excel 2007 Environment

The New User Interface

When you open Excel 2007, or any of the other Office 2007 applications, you will notice that the program interface has changed quite dramatically.

The menu and toolbar design of previous versions of Excel have been replaced, as the program now does a lot more than older versions. The old features have been replaced with a new user interface to make it easier to find and use all the available commands and features. 'Pick and Click' is now the order of the day.

The Ribbon

Traditional menus and toolbars have been replaced by the Ribbon – a new device that presents commands organised into a set of tabs.

The tabs on the Ribbon display the commands that are most relevant for each of the task areas in the application, called groups, as shown for Excel 2007 in Fig. 2.1 on the next page.

Note: To see all the groups available on the Ribbon you must maximise the Excel window. If you reduce the width of the window the Ribbon shrinks, group icons reduce in size and eventually disappear from view.

Fig. 2.1 The Excel 2007 Ribbon.

Context sensitive tabs also appear when they are needed so that you can very easily find and use the commands needed for the current operation. As an example, in Excel 2007, clicking on a chart displays the **Chart Tools** button on the Ribbon which when clicked displays further tabs for changing the design, layout and format of a chart. On leaving the chart, these tabs disappear.

Fig. 2.1 above also shows two of the other new features common to all Office 2007 application, namely the **Microsoft Office** button, and the **Quick Access Toolbar** button, which will be discussed shortly.

Components of the Ribbon

There are four basic components to the Ribbon:

Tabs – There are seven basic tabs across the top, each representing an activity area.

Groups – Each tab has several groups that show related items together.

Commands – A command is a button.

Dialogue Box Launcher – Many groups have an arrow icon 🔲 in the lower-right corner to open an 'old style' dialogue box.

The Components of a ribbon are shown in Fig. 2.2 below.

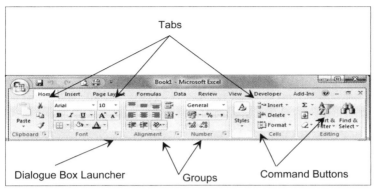

Fig. 2.2 The Components of a Ribbon.

The Home Tab

For each application the Home tab contains all the things you use most often, such as the **Cut** and **Paste** commands and those used for formatting, and for changing text font, size, bold, italic, and so on. Clicking a new tab opens a new series of groups, each with its relevant command buttons. This really works very well.

The Ribbon is scalable, and adapts to different sized screens. It displays smaller versions of tabs and groups as screen resolution decreases. When you make the Ribbon smaller, the groups on the open tab begin to shrink horizontally. The most commonly used commands or features are left open as the program window shrinks. Excel 2007 is probably best used with large high resolution screens, but there again, so is almost everything else in computing!

Dialogue Box Launcher

The new Ribbon holds the most commonly used command buttons for Excel 2007, but by no means all of the available commands. Some groups have a small diagonal arrow in the lower-right corner.

This is the new **Dialogue Box Launcher**. You click it to see more options related to that group. They often appear as a Dialogue box similar to those of previous versions of Excel, as shown in Fig. 2.3 below.

Fig. 2.3 The Font Tab Screen of the Format Cells Dialogue Box.

This was opened by clicking the **Dialogue Box Launcher** located on the **Font** group of the **Home** tab of the Excel 2007 Ribbon.

To confuse matters slightly, some Dialogue Box Launchers actually open task panes, not dialogue boxes. Try clicking the Launcher on Excel 2007's **Home**, **Clipboard** group, to see what we mean.

Contextual Tabs

Not all of the available tabs are visible. Some only appear when they are needed.

As an example, in Excel 2007, clicking on a shape inserted previously in a document, opens a contextual tab on the Ribbon with commands used for editing a shape, as shown in Fig. 2.4 below. Once you leave the shape, by clicking outside it, this **Drawing Tools** tab disappears. Very clever.

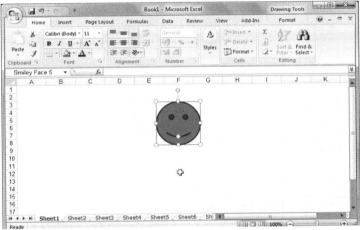

Fig. 2.4 Excel 2007's Contextual Drawing Tools Tab.

Hiding the Ribbon

The Ribbon makes everything in Excel 2007 centralised and easy to find, but there are times when you just want to work on your document.

You can maximise your working area by hiding the Ribbon. To do this just double-click the active tab. All the groups just disappear. Go on, try it. When you want to see the commands again, double-click the active tab to bring back the groups.

If you find you hate the Ribbon in Excel 2007, you have a problem as there is no easy way to delete or replace it with the toolbars and menus from the earlier versions.

Ribbon Keyboard Shortcuts

Those of you who have trouble using a mouse will be glad to hear that all the Ribbon features are available from the keyboard using what are now called **Key Tips**.

Pressing the **Alt** key makes **Key Tip** badges appear for all Ribbon tabs, the **Quick Access** toolbar commands, and the **Office Button** (see Fig. 2.5).

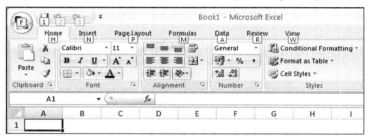

Fig. 2.5 Excel 2007 Ribbon Showing Key Tips.

Then you can press the **Key Tip** for the tab you want to display. If that tab is the active one, all the Key Tips for the tab's commands appear, as we show in Fig. 2.6 below, where we pressed the 'H' keyboard key. Then you can press the **Key Tip** for the command you want.

Fig. 2.6 Excel 2007's Home Tab Key Tips.

When you press a **Key Tip** for a non-active tab, the tab is opened and all the **Key Tips** for the tab's commands appear. Access keys let you quickly use commands by pressing a few keystrokes, no matter where you are in the program. Press the **Alt** key again to close them.

You can still use the old **Alt+** shortcuts that accessed menus and commands in previous versions of Office applications, but because the old menus are no longer available you need to know the full shortcuts to use them. Shortcuts that start with the **Ctrl** key, such as **Ctrl+C** for copy, remain the same as in previous versions.

The Microsoft Office Button

The Microsoft **Office Button** replaces the **File** menu of previous Excel versions (as it does with most other Office applications) and is located in the upper-left corner of the main Excel program window.

Fig. 2.7 The Office Button Menu.

When you click this button you see commands to **Open**, **Save**, **Send** and **Print** your file, as well as new commands such as **Prepare**, and **Publish**. In Excel, by pointing to **Prepare**, and then clicking **Inspect Document**, you can check a file for hidden meta data or personal information. The right side of the menu lists recently opened documents, and gives access to the application's control options.

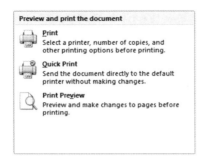

Fig. 2.8 The Print Sub-Menu.

Hovering the mouse pointer over the **Print** button of Fig. 2.7, opens a sub-menu, as shown in Fig. 2.8, giving easy access to your printer controls.

To change settings in previous versions of Excel, you had to click **Options** on the **Tools** menu. Now, all these settings are part of the Excel Options window which you open (see Fig. 2.9) by clicking the **Excel Options** button shown here and at the bottom of Fig. 2.7.

Fig. 2.9 The Excel Options Dialogue Box.

This dialogue box lets you change any of Excel 2007's settings and defaults.

The Quick Access Toolbar

The **Quick Access** toolbar is the small area to the upper left of the Ribbon next to the **Office Button**, pointed to in Fig. 2.1 and shown here. This bar contains buttons for the things that you use over and over every day, such as **Save**, **Undo**, and **Redo**.

To add other commands to the **Quick Access** toolbar, click the **Customize Quick Access Toolbar** button ⬇ and select the **More Commands** from the drop-down menu. This opens the Excel Options window shown in Fig. 2.10 below.

Fig. 2.10 Customising the Quick Access Toolbar.

To add a command to the **Quick Access** toolbar, select it in the left pane and click the **Add** button. To remove it just do the opposite. You can change the position of a new button by selecting it in the right pane and clicking the up and down arrows . To finish, click the **OK** button.

The Mini Toolbar

Some text formatting commands are so useful that you want to have them immediately available without having to go to any of the tabs on the Ribbon. For these, Excel 2007 shows a 'hovering' **Mini** toolbar over your work as shown here.

In this example, we typed some text in an Excel cell and wanted to quickly format it. We selected it by dragging the mouse pointer over the text we wanted to format, then pointed at the selection. A faded **Mini** toolbar appeared, which when pointed to became solid, as shown above. A **Mini** toolbar will stay active for a selection until you click outside the selection.

The Right-click Menu

In Excel, the **Mini** toolbar displays a rather limited formatting choice. A much larger choice of formatting and other commands is available to you by right-clicking a cell, as shown in Fig. 2.11. These menu options, however, are applicable to the entire content of a cell, so high-lighting part of the text is not necessary. If you do, right-clicking a highlighted selection displays only the rather limited **Mini** toolbar.

Fig. 2.11 The Right-click Menu.

Galleries

Galleries are at the heart of the redesigned 'Pick and Click' Excel 2007, as they are also with the other Office applications. Galleries provide you with a set of clear visual results to choose from when you are working in a workbook. By presenting a simple set of potential results, rather than a complex dialogue box with numerous options, Galleries simplify the process of producing good looking work. As we have seen, dialogue boxes are still available if you want more control over an operation, but a simple Gallery choice will very often be enough.

Fig. 2.12 A Style Gallery in Excel 2007.

As we show above, you can apply pre-set orientation of text in a cell from the appropriate gallery in the Ribbon. In Fig. 2.12 we show the result of clicking the **Rotate Text Down** option in the Gallery.

Live Preview

Live Preview is a new feature to Excel and other Office 2007 applications. It previews the results of applying an editing or formatting change as you move the pointer over the options in a Gallery.

In our example in Fig. 2.13 below, as we moved the pointer over the font style options in the gallery, the cell text automatically changed to show how it would look if that style were chosen.

Fig. 2.13 A Live Preview of a Gallery Style in Excel 2007.

Excel 2007 File Formats

Excel 2007, like other Office applications, now uses the Microsoft Office Open XML file formats, based on Extensible Markup Language (XML). File extensions change from **.xls** to **.xlsx**. If you are saving a file with macros, the extension changes again to **.xlsxm**, so you know if the file contains macros or not.

The full range of Excel's file extensions is as follows:

XML file type Extension Workbook	.xlsx
Macro-enabled workbook	.xlsm
Template	.xltx
Macro-enabled template	.xltm
Non-XML binary workbook	.xlsb
Macro-enabled add-in	.xlam

XML files have practical advantages. Each file is actually a zip file of individual elements. If your file gets corrupted, it's easier to recover more of the data. They are compressed to around half the size of standard files.

If you need to, you can still save your files in the older Excel formats with the **Save As** command, but all the .XML advantages will be lost.

Excel 2007 can open files created in all previous versions of Excel in 'compatibility' mode. You know this because at the top of the document "(Compatibility Mode)" appears next to the name of the file. You can then convert the older document to the new file format by clicking the Microsoft Office Button, and selecting the **Convert** command on the drop-down menu.

The new file format also gives you the ability to use features that are available only in Excel 2007. One example of such a feature is the new SmartArt Graphics. The new file format supports plenty of other new features, such as math equations, themes, and content controls.

The Mouse Pointers

In Microsoft Excel, as with all other graphical based programs, using a mouse makes many operations both easier and more fun to carry out.

Excel 2007 makes use of the mouse pointers available in Windows, some of the most common of which are illustrated below. When Microsoft Excel is initially started up the first thing you will see is the rotating circle in Windows Vista or the hourglass in Windows XP, which turns into an upward pointing hollow arrow once the individual application screen appears on your display. Other shapes depend on the type of work you are doing at the time.

- The rotating Vista circle which displays when you are waiting while performing a function.

- The XP hourglass which displays when you are waiting while performing a function.

- The arrow which appears when the pointer is placed over menus, scrolling bars, and buttons.

- The I-beam which appears in normal text areas of the screen. For additional 'Click and Type' pointer shapes, specific to Office applications, see the table overleaf.

- The 4-headed arrow which appears when you choose to move a table, a chart area, or a frame.

↔   The double arrows which appear when over the border of a window, used to drag the side and alter the size of the window.

🖑   The Help hand which appears in the Help windows, and is used to access 'hypertext' type links.

Excel 2007, like other Windows packages, has additional mouse pointers which facilitate the execution of selected commands. Some of these are:

↓   The vertical pointer which appears when pointing over a column in a worksheet and used to select the column.

➡   The horizontal pointer which appears when pointing at a row in a worksheet and used to select the row.

✛   The hollow cross which appears when the pointer is placed within the worksheet area.

◄╫►   The vertical split arrow which appears when pointing over the area separating two columns and used to size a column.

≑   The horizontal split arrow which appears when pointing over the area separating two rows and used to size a row.

+   The cross which you drag to extend or fill a series.

Some Excel operations display the **Help** ⓘ button which when clicked displays the Excel Help screen.

3

The Excel 2007 Spreadsheet

The Excel 2007 Screen

To examine the Excel screen more closely, start Excel 2007, unless already running, by using the **Start**, **All Programs** command, clicking the **Microsoft Office** entry, then clicking the **Microsoft Office Excel 2007** option on the drop-down sub-menu, as discussed in Chapter 1 (page 8), and also shown below in Fig. 3.1 for completeness.

Another way of starting Excel is to double-click on an Excel worksheet file in a Windows folder, in which case the worksheet will be loaded into Excel at the same time.

Fig. 3.1 Using the Start Menu.

When Excel is loaded, it displays an empty and untitled book (Book1) with the **Home** Ribbon selected, as shown in Fig. 3.2 on the next page. The layout, as shown, is in a window, but if you click on the application **Restore** button, you can make Excel take up the full screen area available.

Working in a smaller window can be useful when you are running several **Office** applications at the same time and you want to transfer between them with the mouse.

Fig. 3.2 The Opening Excel Workbook Window.

It is perhaps worth looking at the various parts that make up the above screen. Excel follows the usual Microsoft Windows conventions which hopefully you should be familiar with by now.

Below we describe the screen areas specific to Excel.

Area	*Function*
Name box	Identifies the selected cell (by name or by cell co-ordinates), chart item, or drawing object.
Formula Bar	Can display a number, a label, or the formula behind a result.
Expand Formula Bar	Click to expand the Formula Bar.
Insert Function	Click to open the Insert Function dialogue box.
Select All Button	Click to select the whole worksheet.
Cell pointer	Marks the current cell.
Column letter	The letter that identifies each column.
Row number	The number that identifies each row.
Tab Scrolling Buttons	Clicking on these buttons, scrolls sheet tabs right or left, when there are more tabs than can be displayed at once.
Insert Worksheet	Click to insert another worksheet.
Current sheet	Shows the current sheet amongst a number of sheets in a file.

| | The sheets are named Sheet1, Sheet2, Sheet3, and so on, by default, but can be changed to, say, North, South, East, and West by double-clicking on their current name and typing the new name. Clicking on a sheet tab, moves you to that sheet. |
| Tab split box | The split box which you drag left to see more of the scroll bar, or right to see more tabs. |

Finally, note the location of the horizontal and vertical split boxes by referring to Fig. 3.2. Both of these split the screen and their use will be discussed later.

The Ribbon Tabs

When you first use Excel 2007 the **Home** Ribbon tab is selected by default (see page 16 for a general description of the Ribbon components). Excel's Ribbon has seven tabs, each one with the most used controls grouped on it for the main program actions.

The **Home** tab contains groups for the more common worksheet activities. The Clipboard Cut and Paste commands, Font, Alignment, Number Styles and Cells groups for manipulating cells and their contents, and Editing for other worksheet tasks.

Fig. 3.3 The Home Tab of the Excel 2007 Ribbon.

Clicking the **Insert** tab opens a new series of groups, each with its relevant command buttons, as shown in Fig. 3.4.

Fig. 3.4 The Insert Tab of the Excel 2007 Ribbon.

Under the **Insert** tab, are groupings to enable you to immediately insert Tables, Illustrations, Charts, Links, and Text based features.

The **Page Layout** tab groups controls for you to set your Themes, Page Setup, Scale to Fit, Sheet Options and to Arrange and group sheets, as shown in Fig. 3.5.

Fig. 3.5 The Page Layout Tab of the Excel 2007 Ribbon.

The **Formulas** tab, shown in Fig. 3.6, is for adding and controlling formulae, consisting of a Function Library, Defined Names, Formula Auditing and sheet Calculation options.

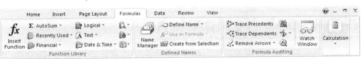

Fig. 3.6 The Formulas Tab of the Excel 2007 Ribbon.

The **Data** tab, shown in Fig. 3.7 on the next page, groups the actions used for handling and analysing your data. These include Get External Data from various sources, Connections for handling external links, Sort & Filter selected data, Data Tools and working with an Outline so that joined cells can be collapsed and expanded.

Fig. 3.7 The Data Tab of the Excel 2007 Ribbon.

The **Review** tab (Fig. 3.8) groups controls for Proofing your worksheets and to initiate and track document review and approval processes. It lets you deal with Comments, and control how Changes made to a worksheet will be handled.

Fig. 3.8 The Review Tab of the Excel 2007 Ribbon.

The **View** tab controls what you see on the screen. You can choose between Worksheet Views, Show or Hide screen features, Zoom to different magnifications, control Windows and run and record Macros.

Fig. 3.9 The View Tab of the Excel 2007 Ribbon.

Workbook Navigation

When you first enter Excel, it sets up a series of worksheets, in your computer's memory, many times larger than the small part shown on the screen. Individual cells are identified by column and row location (in that order), with present size extending to 16,384 columns and 1,048,576 rows. The columns are labelled from A to Z, followed by AA to AZ, BA to BZ, and so on, to XFD, while the rows are numbered from 1 to 1048576.

The point where a row and column intersect is called a cell, and the reference points of a cell are known as the cell address. The active cell (A1 at first) is boxed.

With the large increase in the possible size of Excel 2007's worksheets, finding your way around them is even more important than it used to be. There are four main ways, key combinations, the **Go To** box, scrolling with the mouse, or using the scroll bars.

Key Combinations

To Scroll	*Press*
To the start and end of ranges	**Ctrl+**→, ←, ↓ or ↑ to scroll to the start and end of each range in a column or row before stopping at the end of the worksheet.
One row up or down	**Scroll Lock**, then ↑ or ↓.
One column left or right	**Scroll Lock**, then ← or →.
One window up or down	**PgUp** or **PgDn**.
One window left or right	**Scroll Lock**, then **Ctrl**← or **Ctrl**→.
A large distance	**Scroll Lock+Ctrl+**→, ←, ↓ or ↑.

Pressing the arrow keys while **Scroll Lock** is on will scroll one row up or down or one column left or right.

To use the arrow keys to move between cells, you must turn **Scroll Lock** off.

Pressing the **F5** function key will display the **Go To** dialogue box shown in Fig. 3.10.

In the **Go to** box a list of named ranges in the active worksheet (to be discussed shortly) is displayed, or one of the last four references from which you chose the **Go To** command.

In the **Reference** text box you type the cell reference or a named range you want to move to.

Fig. 3.10 The Go To Box.

To move the active cell with a mouse, do the following:

Point to the cell you want to move to and click the left mouse button. If the cell is not visible, move the window by clicking on the scroll bar arrowhead that points in the direction you want to move,

To move a page at a time, click inside the scroll bar.

For larger moves, drag the box in the scroll bar, but the distances moved will depend on the size of the worksheet.

When you have finished navigating around the worksheet, press the **Ctrl+Home** key combination which will move the active cell to the A1 position (provided you have not fixed titles in any rows or columns or have no hidden rows or columns – more about these later).

Note that the area within which you can move the active cell is referred to as the working area of the worksheet, while the letters and numbers in the border at the top and left of the working area give the 'co-ordinates' of the cells in a worksheet.

The location of the active cell is constantly monitored by the 'selection indicator' in the Name Box which is to be found on the extreme left below the Ribbon. As the active cell is moved, this indicator displays its address, as shown in Fig. 3.11 below.

Fig. 3.11 The Selection Indicator and Formula Bar.

The contents of a cell are displayed above the column letters within what is known as the 'Formula Bar'. If you type text in the active cell, what you type appears in both the Formula Bar and the cell itself.

Typing a formula which is preceded by the equals sign (=) to, say, add the contents of three cells, causes the actual formula to appear in the Formula Bar, while the result of the actual calculation appears in the active cell when the **Enter** key is pressed.

Moving Between Sheets

You can scroll between worksheets by clicking one of the 'Tab scrolling buttons' situated to the left of Sheet1, as shown below.

Fig. 3.12 Tab Scrolling Buttons and the Active Sheet.

The inner arrows scroll sheets one at a time in the direction of the arrow, while the outer arrows scroll to the end, or beginning, of the group of available worksheets. A worksheet is then made current by clicking its tab.

With the keyboard, you can scroll one sheet at a time, and make it active at the same time, by using the **Ctrl+PgDn** key combination. Using **Ctrl+PgUp** scrolls in the reverse direction.

To display more sheet tabs at a time, drag the Tab split box to the right, or to the left to display less sheet tabs. To rename sheets, double-click on their tab, then type the new name to replace the highlighted name.

Fig. 3.13 Right-click Context Menu.

To insert a sheet, click the **Insert Worksheet** button and drag the new tab to where you want it in the stack (see the next section below).

To delete a sheet, right-click on its tab and select **Delete** from the context menu shown in Fig. 3.13. As you can see, you can also **Insert**, **Rename** and **Move** or **Copy** sheets this way.

Rearranging Sheet Order

If you need to rearrange the order in which sheets are being held in a workbook, you can do so by dragging a particular sheet to its new position, as shown in Fig. 3.14.

Fig. 3.14 Moving an Active Sheet.

While you are dragging the tab of the sheet you want to move, the mouse pointer changes to an arrow pointing to a sheet. The small solid arrowhead to the left of the mouse pointer indicates the place where the sheet you are moving will be placed.

Grouping Worksheets

You can select several sheets to group them together so that data entry, editing, or formatting can be made easier and more consistent.

To select adjacent sheets, click the first sheet tab, hold down the **Shift** key and then click the last sheet tab in the group. To select non-adjacent sheets, click the first sheet tab, hold down the **Ctrl** key and then click the other sheet tabs you want to group together.

Selecting sheets in the above manner, causes the word '[Group]' to appear in the Title bar of the active window, and the tabs of the selected sheets to be shown in white. To cancel the selection, right-click a group tab and select **Ungroup Sheets**, or click the tab of any sheet which is not part of the selected group.

Selecting a Range of Cells

To select a range of cells, say, A3:C3, point to cell A3, then:

- Press the left mouse button, and holding it pressed, drag the mouse to the right, as shown below.

Fig. 3.15 Selecting a Range of Cells.

To select a range from the keyboard, first make active the first cell in the range, then:

- Hold down the **Shift** key and use the right arrow key (→) to highlight the required range.

To select a 3D range, across several sheets, select the range in the first sheet, then release the mouse button, hold down the **Shift** key, and click the Tab of the last sheet in the range.

Remember that while a range of cells in a sheet is selected, or a group of sheets is active, pressing the right mouse button displays a shortcut menu with the most common commands relevant to what you are doing at the time, as described in Chapter 2, page 24.

Viewing Multiple Workbook Sheets

To see more clearly what you are doing when working with multiple workbook sheets, click the **Insert Worksheet** button to add a fourth sheet to your Workbook. This, by default, will be named Sheet4, unless you have added more sheets in your current session.

Then click the **View** tab on the Ribbon and click the **Window**, **New Window** command button three times to add three extra windows to your worksheet. To see them, use the **View**, **Window**, **Arrange All**, **Tiled** command to display the four sheets as shown in Fig. 3.16 on the next page. Finally, type the text '1st' in location A1 of Sheet1 of window 1, the text '2nd' in location A1 of Sheet2 of window 2, and so on. What we have done here is to make active Sheet1 in Book1:1, Sheet2 in Book1:2, and so on, to demonstrate that each window contains all four sheets.

Fig. 3.16 Multiple Workbook Sheets in Tile View.

The top left window is the active one above. To move from one window to another, simply point with the mouse to the cell of the window you want to go to and click the left mouse button. To display a different sheet in each window, go to a window and click the sheet's tab.

Fig. 3.17

To return to single-window view from a tiled or cascade mode, click the maximise button of the active window.

You can then use the **View**, **Window**, **Switch Windows** button, shown in Fig. 3.17, to see what windows are open and to move between them. To close an active window, click its **Close** button.

Entering Information

We will now investigate how information can be entered into a worksheet. But first, make sure you are in Sheet1, then return to the Home (A1) position, by pressing the **Ctrl+Home** key combination, then type the words:

   `Project Analysis`

As you type, the characters appear in both the 'Formula Bar' and the active cell. If you make a mistake, press the **BkSp** key to erase the previous letter or the **Esc** key to start again. When you have finished, press **Enter** to move to the cell below, or the **Tab** key to move to the next cell to the right.

Note that what you have just typed in has been entered in cell A1, even though the whole of the word 'Analysis' appears to be in cell B1. If you use the right arrow key to move the active cell to B1 you will see that the cell is indeed empty.

Typing any letter at the beginning of an entry into a cell results in a 'text' entry being formed automatically, otherwise known as a 'label'. If the length of the text is longer than the width of a cell, it will continue into the next cell to the right of the current active cell, provided that cell is empty, otherwise the displayed information will be truncated.

To edit information already in a cell, either

- double-click the cell in question, or
- make that cell the active cell and press the **F2** function key.

The cursor keys, the **Home** and **End** keys, as well as the **Ins** and **Del** keys can be used to move the cursor and/or edit information as required.

You can also 'undo' the last 16 actions carried out since the program was last in the **Ready** mode, using the **Undo** button ⟲▾ on the Quick Access toolbar (see page 23), or the **Ctrl+Z** keyboard shortcut.

Next, move the active cell to B3 and type

`Jan`

Pressing the right arrow key (→) will automatically enter the typed information into the cell and also move the active cell one cell to the right, in this case to C3. Now type

`Feb`

and press **Enter**.

The looks of a worksheet can be enhanced somewhat by using different types of borders around specific cells. To do this, first select the range of cells, then click the down arrow of the **Home**, **Font**, **Borders** button which, as shown here, opens an extensive list of border types. In our example, we

Fig. 3.18 The Border Button.

have selected the cell range A3:C3, then we chose the **Top and Double Bottom Border** option from the display table.

Next, move to cell A4 and type the label **Income**, then enter the numbers **14000** and **15000** in cells B4 and C4, respectively, as shown in Fig. 3.19 on the next page, but note that by default the labels **Jan** and **Feb** are left justified, while the numbers are right justified.

Fig. 3.19 Default Justification of Labels and Numbers.

Changing Text Alignment and Fonts

Fig. 3.20 The Alignment Group.

One way of improving the looks of this worksheet is to also right justify the text **Jan** and **Feb** within their respective cells. To do this, move the active cell to B3 and select the range B3 to C3 by dragging the mouse, then click the **Home**, **Alignment**, **Align Text Right** button, shown here.

For more control you can use the Format Cells dialogue box shown in Fig. 3.21 below. This is opened by clicking the **Alignment** Dialogue Box Launcher.

Fig. 3.21 Formatting Cells using the Alignment Tab Sheet.

In the Alignment tab sheet select **Right (Indent)** in the **Horizontal** drop-down list and press the **OK** button.

No matter which method you choose, the text items should now appear right justified within their cells. The second method is lengthier, but it provides you with greater flexibility in displaying text, both in terms of position and orientation.

We could further improve the looks of our worksheet by choosing a different font size for the heading **Project Analysis**.

Fig. 3.22 The Font Group.

To achieve this, select cell A1, then click on the down arrow against the **Home**, **Font**, **Font Size** button on the Ribbon, to reveal the band of available point sizes for the selected font. From this band, choose 14, then click both the **Bold** and **Italic** buttons, shown in Fig. 3.22 above.

Fig. 3.23 Setting Currency Format.

Finally, since the numbers in cells B4 to C4 represent money, it would be better if these were prefixed with the £ sign. To do this, select the cell range B4:C4, and click the **Home**, **Number**, **Accounting Number Format** button, shown here in Fig. 3.23, and select **£ English (U.K.)**.

The numbers within the chosen range will now be displayed in currency form, and the width of the cells will automatically adjust to accommodate them, if they are too long which is the case in our example.

To see the actual new width of, say column C, place the mouse pointer to the right of the column letter on the dividing line. When the mouse pointer changes to the shape shown here in Fig. 3.24, press the

Fig. 3.24 Finding the Width of a Cell.

left mouse button without moving the mouse. The cell width will then display within a pop-up text box as 81 pixels, increased from the default column width of 64 pixels. To widen the cells, place the mouse pointer in between the column letters, and drag the pointer to the right, until the width of the column displays as 82 pixels, which also happens to be 11 characters wide.

Saving a Workbook

Now, let's assume we want to stop at this point, but would like to save the work entered so far before leaving the program. First, it's a good idea to return to the Home position by pressing **Ctrl+Home**. This is good practice because the position of the cell pointer at the time of saving the file is preserved.

The quickest way to save a document to disc is to click the **Save** button on the **Quick Access** toolbar.

The usual way however is from the **Office Button** menu, shown in Fig. 3.25 on the next page, which gives you more control of the saving operation.

Fig. 3.25 Saving Operations from the Office Button.

Select the **Save As**, **Excel Workbook** options shown above which opens the Save As dialogue box shown in Fig. 3.26 below.

Fig. 3.26 The Save As Dialogue Box.

We have selected to save our work in the folder **Excel 2007 WorkBooks** we created in our D: drive. You could choose to create this folder within your **Documents** folder on your C: drive by navigating there, then using the **Organize**, **New Folder** command.

To save our work, we selected the newly created folder in the **Address Bar** of the Save As dialogue box, then moved the cursor into the **File name** box, and typed **Project 1**. We suggest you do the same. The file will be saved in the default file type *Excel Workbook*, as displayed in the **Save as type** box. Excel adds the file extension **.xlsx** automatically and uses it to identify it.

Fig. 3.27 File Saving Formats.

By clicking the **Save as type** button at the bottom of the Save As dialogue box, you can save your work in a variety of other formats, including Web Page (html), Template (xltx), and earlier versions of Excel, as shown in Fig. 3.27.

If you want to create backup files or provide password protection to your file, click the down-arrow against the **Tools** button at the bottom of the Save As dialogue box, and select **General Options** from the displayed drop-down menu. This opens the General Options box, shown in the composite Fig. 3.28. Fill in this dialogue box appropriately, press the **OK** button, then click the **Save** button.

Fig. 3.28 The Tools Menu and the General Options Box.

Opening a Workbook

Fig. 3.29 Part of
Office Button Menu.

To open a previously saved
worksheet in Excel you click the
Open button on the **Office
Button** menu, shown here in
Fig. 3.29, or use the **Ctrl+O**
keyboard shortcut. Both launch
the Open dialogue box, shown in Fig. 3.30 below.
Excel asks for a filename to open, with the default *All
Excel Files* being displayed.

Fig. 3.30 The Open Dialogue Box.

To open our previously saved example file
Project 1.xlsx, double-click the **Excel 2007
Workbooks** folder and select it by clicking its name in
the list box, then click the **Open** button.

If you want to change the logged drive, select a new
drive in the **Address Bar**.

The last few files you worked on are also listed next to the **Office Button** menu, as shown in Fig. 3.29 on the previous page. Selecting one of these will reopen that file. If you haven't saved it, don't worry as you could just as easily start afresh.

Exiting Excel

To exit Excel, close any displayed dialogue boxes by clicking the **Cancel** button, and make sure that the word **Ready** is displayed on the status bar (press the **Esc** key until it does), and use one of the following methods:

- Use the **Alt+F4** keyboard shortcut.
- Click the **Close** button at the top right of the Excel window.
- Click **Exit Excel** on the **Office Button** menu.

No matter which command you choose, if you have changed any opened worksheet, Excel will warn you and will ask for confirmation before exiting the program, as follows.

Fig. 3.31 An Excel Warning Box.

If you do not want to save the changes, then press the **No** button, otherwise press **Yes**.

4

Filling in a Worksheet

As an example of how a worksheet can be built up, we will use the few entries on 'Project Analysis' from the previous chapter. As we have seen, to open a previously saved worksheet in Excel you first click the **Office Button** , then you select it from the **Recent Documents** list. If it isn't there, click the **Open** button and in the displayed dialogue box navigate to the folder in which you saved **Project 1** in the first place. If you haven't saved it, don't worry as you could just as easily start afresh.

Our aim is to build the worksheet shown in Fig. 4.1. For how to do this and formatting details see next page.

Fig. 4.1 Entering Data in Project 1 Worksheet.

To edit existing entries in a worksheet, either double-click on the contents of a cell then change them, or simply retype the contents of cells to replace them, so that your worksheet looks as similar as possible to the one in Fig. 4.1, on the previous page.

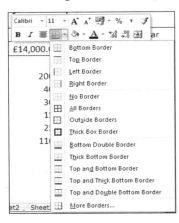

The lines, like the double line at the bottom of the A3 to E3 and A4 to E4 ranges were entered by first selecting each range, then right-clicking it and using the **Borders** button on the Mini Toolbar that hovers over the selection, as shown in Fig. 4.2. A super feature, this!

Fig. 4.2 The Mini Toolbar.

You can also use the Ribbon by clicking the down-arrow of the **Home**, **Font**, **Borders** button, and selecting the appropriate border from the same drop-down list options.

Formatting Entries

Fig. 4.3 Home, Font Group.

The information in cell A1 (Project Analysis: Adept Consultants Ltd.) was entered left-justified and formatted from the **Home**, **Font** group in Arial from the drop-down **Font** list, 14 from the drop-down **Font Size** list, and then clicking in succession the **Bold** and **Italic** buttons, all as shown in Fig. 4.3.

The text in the cell block B3:E3 was formatted by first selecting the range and then clicking the **Home**, **Alignment**, **Center** command button, shown here, to display the text in the range centre-justified.

The numbers within the cell block B4:E4 were formatted by first selecting the range, then clicking the **Home**, **Number**, **Accounting Number Format** button, shown here, and selecting **£ English (U.K.)** from the drop-down list. By default, this sets the numbers to appear with two digits after the decimal point and prefixed with the £ sign.

All the text appearing in column A (apart from that in cell A1) was just typed in (left justified). The width of all the columns A to E was adjusted to 12 characters; a quick way of doing this is to select one row of these columns, then click the **Home**, **Cells**, **Format** button, select **Column Width** from the menu shown in Fig. 4.4, type 12 in the displayed box, as shown in Fig. 4.5, and click **OK**.

Fig. 4.4 The Format Button.

Fig. 4.5 The Column Width Box.

Filling a Range by Example

To fill a range by example, select the first cell of a range, point at the bottom right corner of the cell and when the mouse pointer changes to a small cross, as

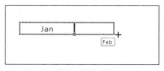

Fig. 4.6 Dragging a Range.

in Fig. 4.6, drag the mouse in the required direction to fill the range.

In this case, we started with a cell containing the abbreviation 'Jan'. The next cell to the right will automatically fill with the text 'Feb' (Excel anticipates that you want to fill cells by example with the abbreviations for months, and does it for you). Not only that, but it also copies the format of the selected range forward.

The Auto Fill Smart Tag

When you release the mouse button, Excel places a Smart Tag next to the end of the filled-in range. Clicking the down-arrow of this Smart Tag displays a drop-down menu of options, as shown in Fig. 4.7.

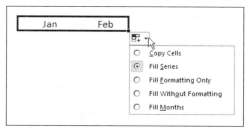

Fig. 4.7 The Auto Fill Smart Tag Options.

Entering Text, Numbers and Formulae

Excel 2007 allows you to format both text (labels) and numbers in any way you choose. For example, you can have numbers centre justified in their cells.

When text, a number, a formula, or an Excel function is entered into a cell, or reference is made to the contents of a cell by the cell address, then the content of the status bar changes from **Ready** to **Enter**. This status can be changed back to **Ready** by either completing an entry and pressing **Enter**, **Tab**, one of the arrow keys, or pressing **Esc**.

We can find the 1st quarter total income from consultancy, by activating cell E4, typing

   =b4+c4+d4

and pressing **Enter**. The total first quarter income is added, using the above formula, and the result (£45,000) is placed in cell E4.

When you have entered everything in Fig. 4.1 click the **Save As** button on the **Office Button** ⓔ menu to save the resultant worksheet under the filename **Project 2**, before going on any further. Remember that saving your work on disc often is a good thing to get used to, as even the shortest power cut can cause the loss of hours of hard work!

Using Functions

In our example, writing a formula that adds the contents of three columns is not too difficult or lengthy a task. But imagine having to add 20 columns! For this reason Excel has an inbuilt summation function which can be used to add any number of columns (or rows).

To illustrate how this and other functions can be used, activate cell E4 and first press **Del** to clear the cell of its formula, then click the **Insert Function** button in the **Function Library** group of the **Formulas** tab, shown here.

If the function you require appears on the displayed dialogue box under **Select a function**, choose it, otherwise type a brief description of what you want to do in the **Search for a function** text box and press **Go**, or select the appropriate class from the list under **Or select a category**.

Fig. 4.8 Selecting a Function.

Choosing the **SUM** function, inserts the entry SUM(B4:D4) in the Formula bar, as shown in Fig. 4.9 on the next page. Clicking the **OK** button, places the result of the calculation of the chosen function in the selected worksheet cell. (E4 in our case).

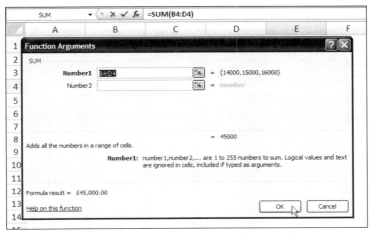

Fig. 4.9 The Function Arguments Dialogue Box.

Note that the arguments in the above case are given as B4:D4 in the **Number1** box and the actual result of the calculation is displayed underneath. Pressing the **OK** button, causes the function to be pasted into cell E4, but only the formula result is displayed in the cell. If you click in the **Number2** box you can select another cell range to be summed. The overall result appears at the bottom of the box.

Using the AutoSum Button

With addition, there is a better and quicker way of letting Excel work out the desired result. To illustrate this, select the cell range B6:E12, which contains the 'Costs' we would like to add up. To add these in both the horizontal and vertical direction, we include in the selected range an empty column to the right of the numbers and an empty row below the numbers, as shown in Fig. 4.10 on the next page.

	A	B	C	D	E	F
1	*Project Analysis: Adept Consultants Ltd.*					
2						
3		Jan	Feb	Mar	1st Quarter	
4	Income	£14,000.00	£15,000.00	£ 16,000.00	£45,000.00	
5	Costs:					
6	Wages	2000	3000	4000		
7	Travel	400	500	600		
8	Rent	300	300	300		
9	Heat/Light	150	200	130		
10	Phone/Fax	250	300	350		
11	Adverts	1100	1200	1300		
12	Total Costs					
13	Profit					
14	Cumulative					
15						

Fig. 4.10 Selecting the Range to be Summed.

Pressing the **Formulas**, **Function Library**, **AutoSum** command button, shown on page 59, inserts the result of the summations in the empty column and row, as shown in Fig. 4.11.

	A	B	C	D	E	F
1	*Project Analysis: Adept Consultants Ltd.*					
2						
3		Jan	Feb	Mar	1st Quarter	
4	Income	£14,000.00	£15,000.00	£ 16,000.00	£45,000.00	
5	Costs:					
6	Wages	2000	3000	4000	9000	
7	Travel	400	500	600	1500	
8	Rent	300	300	300	900	
9	Heat/Light	150	200	130	480	
10	Phone/Fax	250	300	350	900	
11	Adverts	1100	1200	1300	3600	
12	Total Costs	4200	5500	6680	16380	
13	Profit					
14	Cumulative					
15						

Fig. 4.11 The Result of the AutoSum Action.

The selected range remains selected so that any other formatting can be applied by simply pressing the appropriate Ribbon buttons.

Note that the **AutoSum** button now has a down-arrow to the right of it. Clicking this arrow, displays a list of alternative options, as shown in Fig. 4.12. From this list you can choose to calculate the **Average**, **Count Numbers** in the entries, find the **Max** or **Min** values in a row or column, or open the Insert Function dialogue box discussed earlier by selecting the **More Functions** option.

Fig. 4.12
AutoSum Menu.

Now complete the insertion of formulae in the rest of the worksheet, noting that 'Profit', in B13, is the difference between 'Income' and 'Total Cost', calculated by the formula **=b4-b12**. To complete the entry, this formula should be copied using the 'fill by example' method we discussed earlier, into the three cells to its right.

The 'Cumulative' entry in cell B14 should be a simple reference to cell B13, that is **=b13**, while in cell C14 it should be **=b14+c13**. Similarly, the latter formula is copied into cell D14 using the 'fill by example' method.

Next, format the entire range B6:E12 by selecting the range and clicking the **Home, Number, Accounting Number Format** button, shown here, and selecting **£ English (U.K.)**

If you make any mistakes and copy formats or information into cells you did not mean to, use the **Undo** button on the **Quick Access** toolbar, or the **Ctrl+Z** keyboard shortcut. To blank the contents of a range of cells, select the range, then press the **Del** key.

The data in your worksheet, up to this point, should look like that in Fig. 4.13 below.

	A	B	C	D	E	F
1	*Project Analysis: Adept Consultants Ltd.*					
2						
3		Jan	Feb	Mar	1st Quarter	
4	Income	£14,000.00	£15,000.00	£ 16,000.00	£45,000.00	
5	Costs:					
6	Wages	£ 2,000.00	£ 3,000.00	£ 4,000.00	£ 9,000.00	
7	Travel	£ 400.00	£ 500.00	£ 600.00	£ 1,500.00	
8	Rent	£ 300.00	£ 300.00	£ 300.00	£ 900.00	
9	Heat/Light	£ 150.00	£ 200.00	£ 130.00	£ 480.00	
10	Phone/Fax	£ 250.00	£ 300.00	£ 350.00	£ 900.00	
11	Adverts	£ 1,100.00	£ 1,200.00	£ 1,300.00	£ 3,600.00	
12	Total Costs	£ 4,200.00	£ 5,500.00	£ 6,680.00	£ 16,380.00	
13	Profit	£9,800.00	£9,500.00	£9,320.00	£28,620.00	
14	Cumulative	£9,800.00	£19,300.00	£28,620.00		
15						

Fig. 4.13 The Completed 1st Quarter Worksheet.

Finally, use the **Save As** button on the **Office Button** menu to save the resultant worksheet with the filename **Project 3** in your **Excel 2007 WorkBook** folder.

Formulae and Functions

As we have seen, **Formulas** in Excel (or formulae to the rest of us!) are equations that perform calculations on values in your worksheet. A formula starts with an equal sign (=) and can contain any of the following:

- **Functions** – Built in Excel formulas that take a value or values, perform an operation, and return a value or values. You use functions to simplify and shorten worksheet formulas.

- **References** – Addresses of cells in the worksheet.

- **Operators** – Signs or symbols that specify the type of calculation to perform in an expression. Operators can be mathematical, comparison, logical, or reference.

- **Constants** – Values that are not calculated and, therefore, do not change.

Excel Functions

Excel's functions are built-in formulas that perform specialised calculations. Their general format is:

NAME(arg1, arg2, ...)

where **NAME** is the function name, and **arg1**, **arg2**, etc., are the arguments required for the evaluation of the function. Arguments must appear in a parenthesised list as shown above and their exact number depends on the function being used. However, some functions, such as **PI**, do not require arguments and are used without parentheses.

There are four types of arguments used with functions: numeric values, range values, string values and conditions, the type used being dependent on the type of function. Numeric value arguments can be entered either directly as numbers, as a cell address, a cell range name or as a formula. Range value arguments can be entered either as a range address or a range name, while string value arguments can be entered as an actual value (a string in double quotes), as a cell address, a cell name, or a formula. Condition arguments normally use logical operators or refer to an address containing a logic formula.

Excel has many types of functions, including, financial, logical, text, date and time, lookup and reference, mathematical and trigonometric, statistical, database, engineering and information. Each type requires its own number and type of arguments.

To find out in detail about all of Excel 2007's functions go to the **Function reference** section in Excel Help. This gives working examples of everything, but you must be online to receive them. For instant reference, have a look at the **Excel 2007 Functions** chapter at the end of this book.

In Excel 2007 you can use the **Formulas** tab to place and work with formulae and functions. As shown in Fig. 4.14 below, the main function types have their own Ribbon buttons. Just clicking these and pointing to a function on one of their lists, gives a good overview of what the function does and what parameters it needs:

Fig. 4.14 The Formulas, Function Library.

That's enough theory, if you want to go deeper you can study the Help system. In the next section we give an example to show that cell references in formulae can be added automatically by selecting cells or ranges of cells. You don't even have to type them into your formulae.

Building a Formula

You can enter formulas straight into a selected cell, or into the Formula bar, which is now re-sizeable. In Fig. 4.15 we will step through the procedure of building a simple formula in cell E3, to average the contents of cells C2 to C4, or the range (C2:C4).

Fig. 4.15 Building a Simple Formula with a Function.

In 1 above we typed '=a' into cell E3. Excel, expecting a formula, opened the drop-down list for you to select one. This is the new Formula AutoComplete feature which helps you write the proper formula syntax.

We double-clicked on **AVERAGE** and selected the range C2:C4 with the pointer, which as you can see in 2 above, entered the function and the selected range into the formula, with a syntax pop-up below to help. Pressing the **Enter** key completed the operation.   •

The result is shown in the cell and the completed formula in the Formula bar when the cell is selected, as shown in 3 of Fig. 4.15 on the previous page. Microsoft have made function use in this version of Excel as intuitive as possible.

A Quick Printout

Before we tell you any more about worksheets, you might like to print **Project 3** quickly to see how it looks on paper, without bothering with page layout, etc.

The quickest way of printing your work is to load the worksheet you want to print into Excel, click the **Office Button** 🔘, then hover the mouse pointer over the **Print** button to display the screen shown in Fig. 4.16 below.

Fig. 4.16 Print Menu Options.

We prefer to start the printing process by clicking the **Print Preview** button pointed to in Fig. 4.16 above.

This opens the Preview screen shown in Fig. 4.17.

Fig. 4.17 The Print Preview Window.

Use the **Zoom** button to get the best view of your work and, if you are happy with it, click the **Print** button to open the Print screen with the default printer selected. Click the **OK** button to see your spreadsheet on paper, provided your printer is connected.

The idea of **Print Preview** is to make it easy for you to see your work on screen before committing it to paper, thus saving a few trees and a lot of ink!

In the next chapter we will discuss in much more detail how to use the **Print Preview** facility to look at large spreadsheets, how to use **Page Setup** to transform your printout to your liking, and how to use headers and footers. So, don't think that what we have discussed so far here is all there is to previewing and printing your work. There is a lot more to come!

5

Enhancing Worksheets

You can make your work look more professional by adopting various enhancements, such as single and double line cell borders, shading certain cells, and adding meaningful headers and footers.

Using Styles

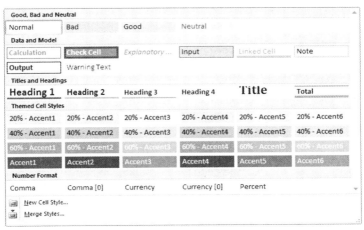

With Excel 2007 it is easy to select from predefined styles to display your work on both the screen and on paper. To do this, select the range you want to format and click the **Home**, **Styles**, **Cell Styles** button shown here which opens the gallery shown below in Fig. 5.1.

Good, Bad and Neutral					
Normal	Bad	Good	Neutral		

Data and Model					
Calculation	Check Cell	Explanatory ...	Input	Linked Cell	Note
Output	Warning Text				

Titles and Headings					
Heading 1	Heading 2	Heading 3	Heading 4	Title	Total

Themed Cell Styles					
20% - Accent1	20% - Accent2	20% - Accent3	20% - Accent4	20% - Accent5	20% - Accent6
40% - Accent1	40% - Accent2	40% - Accent3	40% - Accent4	40% - Accent5	40% - Accent6
60% - Accent1	60% - Accent2	60% - Accent3	60% - Accent4	60% - Accent5	60% - Accent6
Accent1	Accent2	Accent3	Accent4	Accent5	Accent6

Number Format					
Comma	Comma [0]	Currency	Currency [0]	Percent	

New Cell Style...
Merge Styles...

Fig. 5.1 Selecting Cell Styles.

As you move the pointer around this box the selected cells will preview the style effect. To see what appears in Fig. 5.2 below, do the following:

(a) Click cell A1 and reduce the title of the worksheet to 'Project Analysis', then highlight the range A1:E1 and click the **Home**, **Alignment**, **Merge** button, shown here, and select **Merge and Center** to centre the title within the selected range.

(b) Highlight the range A3:A14 and use the **Home**, **Style**, **Cell Styles** and from the themed colours gallery, select the left **Accent1** column.

(c) Highlight the range B43:E:3 and repeat (b) above.

What displays now on your screen should be similar to the screen in Fig.5.2 below.

Fig. 5.2 The Data for the Second Quarter.

Finally, use the **Save As** icon on the **Office Button** menu to save the resultant worksheet with the filename **Project 4** in your **Excel 2007 WorkBook** folder.

Page Layout View

Before you print an Excel worksheet that contains large amounts of data or charts, you can now use the new Page Layout view to visually change the page orientation, add or edit page headers and footers, set printing margins, and hide or display row and column headers. You can also enter and format data as in the Normal view, and use the rulers to measure the width and height of your data.

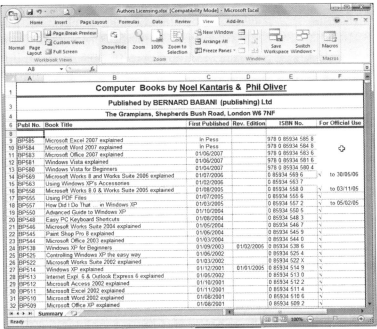

Fig. 5.3 A Worksheet in Page Layout View.

To open Page Layout view either, click the **View**, **Page Layout View** button on the **Workbook Views** group on the Ribbon, or click the **Page Layout View** button 🔲 on the Status bar. To return to Normal view click the **Normal View** button 🔳.

The **Zoom** slider is very useful in this view. You just slide the centre button to the left to show more of the worksheet on the screen and to the right to see less. The magnification % is shown to its left.

Printing a Large Worksheet

Fig. 5.4, The
Page Setup Group.

Before you print from a large worksheet you should check and if necessary change the print settings. Most of the commands for this are in the **Page Layout**, **Page Setup** group shown in Fig. 5.4.

Setting a Print Area

To choose a smaller print area than the current worksheet, select the required area by highlighting the starting cell of the area and dragging the mouse to highlight the block, click the **Print Area** command button selected above, and choose the **Set Print Area** option on the drop-down menu.

Print Preview

Don't forget to preview your work before committing it to paper. To display the Print Preview window, click the **Office Button** 🗈 then hover the mouse pointer over the **Print** button to display the **Print** menu options then click **Print Preview** in the sub-menu as discussed in Chapter 4 (page 66).   You can also click the **Print Preview** button on the Page Setup dialogue box, or the **Preview** button on the Print dialogue box. So many choices to make it easy for you to see your work on screen!

As an example, open the **Project 4** file, and set the print range as A1:E14. Next, open the Print Preview window and click the **Page Setup** button. This opens the box in Fig. 5.5, with the Page tab open

Fig. 5.5 Adjusting Page Settings.

A very useful feature of Excel is the **Scaling** facility shown in the above dialogue box. You can print actual size or a percentage of it, or you can choose to fit your worksheet on to one page which allows Excel to scale your work automatically. We set the **Adjust to % normal size** to 145.

In the **Margins** tab we set the **Center on page** setting to **Horizontally** and moved to the Header/Footer tab as shown in Fig. 5.6 on the next page.

Fig. 5.6 The Header/Footer Tab Settings.

Header and Footer Icons and Codes

Clicking the **Custom Header** button opens the Header box also shown in Fig. 5.7 on the next page.

You can type text into any of the three boxes, or click on one of the buttons. **Sheet Name**, for example, inserts the **&[Tab]** code which has the effect of inserting the sheet name of the current active sheet at the time of printing. The first icon button displays the Font dialogue box, while the others display the following codes:

Code	*Action*
&[Page]	Inserts a page number.
&[Pages]	Inserts the total number of pages.
&[Date]	Inserts the current date.
&[Time]	Inserts the current time.
&[File]	Inserts the filename of the current workbook.

Fig. 5.7 The Header Dialogue Box.

We added the information and code shown above to our example, then clicked the **Show Margins** button in the **Preview** group, to display the screen in Fig. 5.8 below.

Fig. 5.8 The Data for the Second Quarter.

You can use the preview screen in Fig. 5.8 to fine-tune the margins so that the worksheet is centred on the page.

When all is set, clicking the **Print** button on the **Print Preview** Ribbon (or anywhere else for that matter) opens the Print dialogue box shown below.

Fig. 5.9 The Print Dialogue Box.

Here you can choose your printer and its settings. In **Print what** choose **Selection** to print the current selection, **Active sheet(s)** or the **Entire workbook**. If you have included headers and footers, these will be printed out irrespective of whether you choose to print a selected range or a selected worksheet. Clicking **OK** will start the printing operation. Don't forget to check your work in the **Print Layout** mode though, you may save a little heartache!

3-Dimensional Worksheets

In Excel, a Workbook is a 3-dimensional file made up with a series of flat 2-dimensional sheets stacked 'on top of each other'. As mentioned previously, each separate sheet in a file has its own Tab identifier at the bottom of the screen. Ranges can be set to span several different sheets to build up 3-dimensional blocks of data. These blocks can then be manipulated, copied, or moved to other locations in the file. A cell can reference any other cell in the file, no matter what sheet it is on, and an extended range of functions can be used to process these 3-dimensional ranges.

The best way to demonstrate a new idea is to work through an example – we will use the worksheet saved under **Project 4**.

Copying Sheets in a Workbook

We will now fill another three sheets behind the present one, in order to include information about ADEPT Consultants' trading during the other three quarters of the year. The easiest way of doing this is by copying the information in Sheet1, including the formatting and the entered formulae, onto the other three sheets, then edit the numerical information in these appropriately.

To simplify this operation, Excel has a facility which allows you to copy a sheet into a workbook. Although there are two ways of doing this: (a) with the mouse, or (b) from the Ribbon, we find the second method far too elaborate, therefore we only discuss here the first method.

With the mouse, make the sheet you want to copy the current sheet, then press the **Ctrl** key, and while keeping it pressed, point with the mouse on the Tab of Sheet1 and drag it to the right, as shown in Fig. 5.10.

A small black triangle indicates the place where the copy will be inserted, as shown.

Fig. 5.10 Drag Copying a Sheet into a Workbook.

If you insert a copy, say before Sheet2, when you release the mouse button the inserted sheet will be given the name Sheet1(2), while inserting a second copy before Sheet2 will be given the name Sheet1(3). To delete a worksheet, right-click its tab and select **Delete** from the pop-up menu.

If you find the above method too cumbersome, click the Tab of Sheet1 to make it current, press **Ctrl+C** to copy it to the **Clipboard**, then click the Tab of Sheet2 and press **Ctrl+V** to paste the contents of the **Clipboard** into the second sheet.

When you have three copies placed, double-click the Tabs of Sheet1 and the three new sheets and change their names to 'Quarter 1', 'Quarter 2', 'Quarter 3' and 'Quarter 4', respectively, as shown in Fig. 5.11.

The correct contents of the second sheet should be as shown in Fig. 5.11 on the next page. The easiest way to enter these 2nd Quarter results is just to select a cell and type the new value. You can also edit the copied data (from Quarter 1) by either using the EDIT key (**F2**), or double-clicking the cell you want to edit. You should now be in a position to complete the editing of this sheet.

Be extra careful, from now on, to check the identification Tab at the bottom of the window, so as not to get the sheets mixed up. You don't want to spend time editing the wrong worksheet!

Fig. 5.11 The Data for the Second Quarter.

Next, build two additional sheets for the last two quarters of the year (see below for details on the 3rd and 4th quarters).

	Jul	Aug	Sep	Oct	Nov	Dec
Income	17,000	17,500	18,000	18,500	19,000	19,500
Costs:						
Wages	4,000	4,500	5,000	4,500	5,000	5,500
Travel	600	650	680	630	670	700
Rent	300	300	300	300	300	300
Heat/Light	50	80	120	160	200	250
Phone/Fax	350	380	420	400	420	450
Adverts	1,400	1,450	1,500	1,480	1,500	1,530

After building up all four worksheets (one for each quarter) save the file as **Project 5**.

Linking Sheets

Use the **Home**, **Cells**, **Insert** command and click **Insert Sheet** to place a worksheet in front of the 'stack' of data sheets to show a full year's results. Next, make a copy of the 1st Quarter sheet and place it in the new front sheet, then delete the entries in columns B to E, and name it 'Summary'.

We will now link the summary sheet to the other quarterly data sheets so that the information contained on them is automatically summarised and updated on it. The quarter totals in columns E of sheets Quarter 1, Quarter 2,

Quarter 3, and Quarter 4, can be selected and copied in turn using the **Home**, **Clipboard**, **Copy** button, and then pasted to the appropriate column of the summary sheet by selecting the destination range, and clicking the **Paste** button and selecting **Paste Link** as shown in Fig. 5.12.

Fig. 5.12 Pasting Linked Cells.

Note: Empty cells linked with this method, like those in cells E5 of each quarter, appear as 0 (zero) in the Summary sheet. These can be removed with the **Delete** key.

Next, insert appropriate formulae in row 14 to correctly calculate the cumulative values in the Summary sheet. The result should be as shown in Fig. 5.13 on the next page.

Finally, save the resultant workbook as **Project 6**.

Fig. 5.13 Linked Data in the Summary Sheet.

Relative and Absolute Cell Addresses

Entering a mathematical expression into Excel, such as the formula in cell C14 which was

=B14+C13

causes Excel to interpret it as 'add the contents of cell one column to the left of the current position, to the contents of cell one row above the current position'.

In this way, when the formula was later copied into cell address D14, the contents of the cell relative to the left position of D14 (i.e. C14) and the contents of the cell one row above it (i.e. D13) were used, instead of the original cell addresses entered in C14. This is known as relative addressing.

To see the effect of relative versus absolute addressing, copy the formula in cell C14 into C16 using the **Copy** and **Paste** buttons, as shown in Fig. 5.14 on the next page.

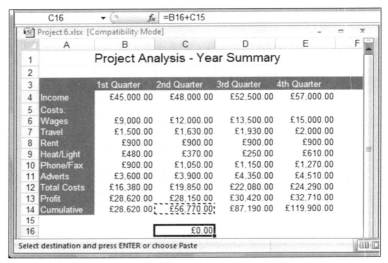

Fig. 5.14 Demonstrating Relative and Absolute Cell Addressing.

Note that in cell C14 the formula was =B14+C13. However, when copied into cell C16 the formula appears as

=B16+C15

This is because it has been interpreted as relative addressing. In this case, no value appears in cell C16 because we are attempting to add two blank cells.

Now change the formula in cell C14 by editing it to

=$B$14+$C$13

which is interpreted as absolute addressing.

Copying this formula into cell C16 calculates the correct result. Highlight cell C16 and observe the cell references in its formula; they have not changed from those of cell C14.

When creating a financial model in a spreadsheet it is common practice to put all the control parameters on a sheet of their own. These might be the $/£ exchange rate, or the % rate of inflation for example. Whenever these parameters are needed in a cell formula in the model they should not just be entered straight into the formula, but absolute references should be made to them in the parameter sheet. In this way you can change a parameter in one place on the parameter sheet and see the overall effects when the model is recalculated.

The $ sign must prefix both the column reference and the row reference. Mixed cell addressing is permitted; as for example when a column address reference is needed to be taken as absolute, while a row address reference is needed to be taken as relative. In such a case, the column letter is prefixed by the $ sign.

When building an absolute cell reference in a formula, it is easier to select each cell address within a formula by double-clicking on it with the left mouse button then, when selected, keep on pressing the **F4** key until the correct $ prefix is set.

Freezing Panes on Screen

With large sheets when you are working in the data area you may not be able to see the label cells associated with that data and it is easy to get very confused.

To get over this you can freeze column (or row) labels of a worksheet on screen so that they are always visible. To do this, move the cell pointer to the right (or below) the column (or row) which you want to freeze, and click the **View**, **Window**, **Freeze Panes** command button shown in Fig. 5.15 on the next page.

Selecting **Freeze Panes** from the drop-down menu will

Fig. 5.15 The Freeze
Panes Button.

place black lines in the sheet to show what is frozen. Then everything to the left of, or above, the cell pointer will freeze on the screen when you scroll through the worksheet.

To unfreeze panes, click the **View**, **Window**, **Freeze Panes** button again and select the **Unfreeze Panes** option. This is only available if you have rows or columns frozen.

Note: In Excel 2007 you cannot use the **View**, **Workbook Views**, **Page Layout** button, pointed to in Fig. 5.16, with frozen panes in your sheet.

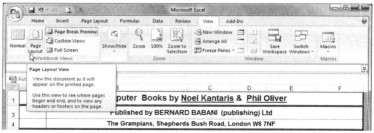

Fig. 5.16 Using the Page Layout Button.

The warning message shown below opens. If you click the **OK** button, the sheet will be unfrozen.

Fig. 5.17 Another Excel Warning Message.

6

Spreadsheet Charts

Excel 2007 makes it very easy to create professional looking charts or graphs from your data – they allow you to graphically display data trends and patterns.

As we shall see, the package can almost instantly create many different chart and graph types, including area, bar, column, line, doughnut, radar, XY, pie, combination, and several 3-D options of these charts. These are made available to you once you have selected the data you want to chart from the **Charts** group on the **Insert** tab.

Charts (you can have several per worksheet) can be displayed on screen at the same time as the worksheet from which they were derived, since they are created in their own chart frame and can be embedded anywhere on a worksheet. They can be sent to an appropriate output device, such as a plotter or printer, or copied to another program such as Word or Powerpoint.

A Simple Column Chart

In order to illustrate some of the graphing capabilities of Excel, we will now plot the income of the consulting company we discussed in the **Project 6** file. However, before we can go on, you will need to complete the entries for the last two quarters of trading of the Adept Consultants' example, if you haven't already done so (see Chapter 5, page 79).

Next, link the quarterly totals to the Summary sheet, and add a column showing the totals for the year, as shown in Figure 6.1, and save the resultant workbook as **Project 7**, before going on.

	F4	▾	f_x =SUM(B4:E4)			
	Project 6.xlsx					– ▫ ✕
	A	B	C	D	E	F
1		Project Analysis - Year Summary				
2						
3		1st Quarter	2nd Quarter	3rd Quarter	4th Quarter	Total
4	Income	£45,000.00	£48,000.00	£52,500.00	£57,000.00	£202,500.00
5	Costs:					
6	Wages	£9,000.00	£12,000.00	£13,500.00	£15,000.00	£49,500.00
7	Travel	£1,500.00	£1,630.00	£1,930.00	£2,000.00	£7,060.00
8	Rent	£900.00	£900.00	£900.00	£900.00	£3,600.00
9	Heat/Light	£480.00	£370.00	£250.00	£610.00	£1,710.00
10	Phone/Fax	£900.00	£1,050.00	£1,150.00	£1,270.00	£4,370.00
11	Adverts	£3,600.00	£3,900.00	£4,350.00	£4,510.00	£16,360.00
12	Total Costs	£16,380.00	£19,850.00	£22,080.00	£24,290.00	£82,600.00
13	Profit	£28,620.00	£28,150.00	£30,420.00	£32,710.00	£119,900.00
14	Cumulative	£28,620.00	£56,770.00	£87,190.00	£119,900.00	£292,480.00
15						
	◄ ◄ ► ►	**Summary** / Quarter 1 / Quarter 2 / Quarter				

Fig. 6.1 The Year's Summary Worksheet for Adept Consultants.

Now we need to select the range of the data we want to graph. In Excel, this range of data does not have to be contiguous for each graph, as with some other spreadsheets. You simply select data from different parts of a sheet with the **Ctrl** key pressed down. This method has the advantage of automatic recalculation should any changes be made to the original data. You could also collect data from different sheets to one 'graphing' sheet by linking them as we did with the summary sheet.

If you don't want the chart to be recalculated when you do this, then you must use the **Home**, **Clipboard**, **Copy** and **Paste**, **Paste Special** command buttons and choose the **Values** option from the displayed dialogue box. This copies a selected range to a specified target area of the worksheet and converts formulae to values.

This is necessary, as cells containing formulae cannot be pasted directly since it would cause the relative cell addresses to adjust to the new locations; each formula would then recalculate a new value for each cell and give wrong results.

Creating a Chart

To obtain a chart of 'Income' versus 'Quarters', select the data in cell range A3..E4, then click the **Insert**, **Charts**, **Column** button, shown below in Fig. 6.2.

Fig. 6.2 Charting Buttons on the Insert Tab.

This opens the drop-down gallery of chart options shown in Fig. 6.3. Now select the **3-D Clustered Column** type and just click it to create the chart shown in Fig. 6.4 on the next page. That's all there is to it, just a few clicks!

Fig. 6.3 The Column Charts Gallery.

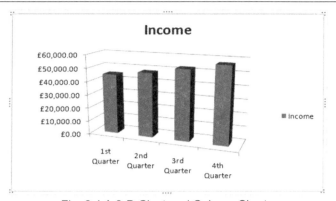

Fig. 6.4 A 3-D Clustered Column Chart.

While the frame containing a chart is selected (you can tell from the presence of the faint blue-green lines around it), you can change its size by dragging the small two-headed arrow pointer (which appears when the mouse pointer is placed on the handles at the corners or middle of the frame). You can also move the frame and its contents to another position on the worksheet by dragging it to a new position.

The Chart Tools

When you select a chart in Excel by clicking it, the **Chart Tools** add the **Design**, **Layout**, and **Format** tabs, as shown below and on the next page.

Fig. 6.5 The Design Tab of the Charting Ribbon.

The Design tab groups controls for you to change the chart Type, Data, Chart Layouts, Chart Styles and Location.

Fig. 6.6 The Layout Tab of the Charting Ribbon.

With the Layout tab you control the layout of the Current Selection, Labels, and Axes, Insert a layout, and Background, Analysis and Properties.

Fig. 6.7 The Format Tab of the Charting Ribbon.

From the Format tab you format the Current Selection, set Shape Styles and WordArt Styles, Arrange objects and Size.

Customising a Chart

Now it is time for you to 'play'. The only way to find out what all the charting controls do is to try them all out. Remember that some options are applied to the chart element that is currently selected, others to the whole chart.

To control what is selected, click the arrow next to the **Chart Elements** box in the **Current Selection** group of the **Format** tab, and then click the chart element that you want, as shown in Fig. 6.8.

Fig. 6.8 The Chart Elements Box.

On the **Layout** tab, we suggest you click the label layout option that you want in the **Labels** group, select what chart axes you want in the **Axes** group, and what layout option you want in the **Background** group.

In the **Current Selection** group, clicking **Format Selection**, opens a Format control box like that shown in Fig. 6.9, in which you select the formatting options you want for the selected chart element.

You can also apply a quick style to individual elements, or use the **Shape Fill**, **Shape Outline**, and **Shape Effects** buttons in the **Shape Quick Styles** group on the **Format** tab. These are our favourite ways of formatting our charts.

Fig. 6.9 Setting Format Options for Chart Elements.

Try it, then change the May income (on the Quarter 2 sheet) from £16,000 to £26,000, and watch how the change is reflected on the redrawn graph. Finally, revert to the original entry for the May income, and if you like, change your chart back to its original column type, and then save your work again under the filename **Project 7** by clicking the **Save** button on the Quick Access toolbar. Your current work will be saved to disc replacing the previous version.

When Excel creates a chart, it plots each row or column of data in the selected range as a 'data series', such as a group of bars, lines, etc. A chart can contain many data series, but Excel charts data according to the following rules:

1. If the selected range contains more rows than columns of data, Excel plots the data series by columns.

2. If the selected range contains more columns than rows of data, or the same number of columns and rows, Excel plots the data series by rows.

If you select a range to chart which includes column and row headings, and text above or to the left of the numeric data, Excel uses the text to create the axis labels, legends, and title.

Saving Charts

When you save a workbook, the chart or charts you have created are saved with it. It is, therefore, a good idea to give each chart a title (select it then use the **Chart Tools**, **Layout** tab, **Properties**, and rename **Chart 1** to **Income Column** and press **Enter**.

It is also a good idea to locate charts on a separate sheet. To do this click the Insert Worksheet tab at the bottom of the screen, move the new sheet in front of the Summary tab and rename it Charts. Use **Cut** and **Paste** to move the chart from its present position to the Charts tab sheet, and save the workbook as **Project 8**.

Predefined Chart Types

To select a different type of chart, click the **Design**, **Type**, **Change Chart Type** button shown here. Excel 2007 uses 11 basic chart types, and with variations of these has 73 type options in all. These chart-types are normally used to describe the following relationships between data:

Area: for showing a volume relationship between two series, such as production or sales, over a given length of time.

Bar: for comparing differences in data (noncontinuous data that are not related over time) by depicting changes in horizontal bars to show positive and negative variations from a given position.

Bubble: for showing a type of XY (scatter) chart. The size of the data (radius of the bubble) indicates the value of a third variable.

Column: for comparing separate items (noncontinuous data which are related over time) by depicting changes in vertical bars to show positive and negative variations from a given position.

Doughnut: for comparing parts with the whole. Similar to pie charts, but can depict more than one series of data.

 Line: for showing continuous changes in data with time.

 Pie: for comparing parts with the whole. You can use this type of chart when you want to compare the percentage of an item from a single series of data with the whole series.

Radar: for plotting one series of data as angle values defined in radians, against one or more series defined in terms of a radius.

 Surface: for showing optimum combinations between two sets of data, as in a topographic map. Colours and patterns indicate areas that are in the same range of values.

Stock: for showing high-low-close type of data variation to illustrate stock market prices or temperature changes.

XY (Scatter): for showing scatter relationships between X and Y. Scatter charts are used to depict items which are not related over time.

Drawing a Multiple Column Chart

As an exercise, we will consider a new column chart which deals with the quarterly 'Costs' of Adept Consultants. To achieve this, first select the Summary sheet of workbook **Project 8**, then highlight the cell range A3:E3, press the **Ctrl** key, and holding it down, use the mouse to select the costs range A6:E11.

Next, click the **Insert**, **Charts**, **Column** button, select Clustered Column from the gallery as pointed to below. The 6 different quarterly costs will be drawn automatically, as displayed in the composite 'before and after' screen dump in Fig. 6.10.

Fig. 6.10 Creating a Costs Column Chart.

Because the selected range contains more rows than columns of data, Excel follows the 1st rule of data series selection, which is not really what we want.

To have the 'quarters' appearing on the x-axis and the 'costs' as the legends, we need to tell Excel that our data series is in rows by clicking the **Design**, **Data**, **Switch Row/Column** button on the Ribbon. In addition, you could enhance the looks of the chart by using the **Layout**, **Background**, **3-D Rotation** options to get the column chart shown in Fig. 6.11 below.

Fig. 6.11 The Costs Column Chart on its own Sheet.

The chart title was added by clicking the **Layout**, **Labels**, **Chart Title** button, selecting **Above Chart** and then typing the heading in the object space provided on the chart. We moved the chart to its own sheet as before and saved the worksheet as **Project 9**.

To see this chart in colour, have a look on the inside of the front cover of the book.

Changing Titles and Labels

To change a title, an axis label, or a legend within a chart, click the appropriate area on the chart. This reveals that these are individual objects (they are surrounded by small green circles and squares called 'handles') and you can edit, reposition, or change their font and point size. You can even rotate text within such areas in any direction you like.

To demonstrate some of these options, we will use the **Costs Column** chart saved in **Project 9**, so get it on screen if you are to follow our suggestions.

To change the font size of a chart title, click in the Chart Title area to select it and select the existing title text. Then simply click the **Home** tab and use any of the **Font** group buttons.

Fig. 6.12 Using Styles.

You can use the options on the **Format**, **WordArt Styles** group to make your chart or axis titles really stand out. To fill text with colour, first click in a title area to select it (see Fig. 6.12), then click the arrow on the **WordArt Styles**, **Text Fill** button to open the colour gallery shown here. With one of our PCs (running Windows XP), the **Auto Preview** feature did not work with the **Theme Colors**; the worksheet did not change as the pointer moved over them, but with another PC (running Windows Vista), the feature works fine. If the **Auto Preview** feature does not work on your PC, you'll just have to click a colour to try it, and use the **Undo** button on the **Quick Access** toolbar if it is not right.

The **WordArt Styles** group also has the **Text Outline** 🖉 and **Text Effects** 🖹 buttons, which include Shadow, Reflection, and Glow effects. The possibilities are almost limitless!

Drawing a Pie Chart

To change the chart type, simply select the chart, click the **Design**, **Type**, **Change Chart Type** button, shown here, and choose from the gallery.

As a last example in chart drawing, we used the data ranges A6:A11 and F6:F11 of the Summary worksheet to plot an **Exploded pie in 3-D** pie chart, as shown below.

Fig. 6.13 A 3-D Pie Expanded Chart.

To display the above chart, we clicked the **Layout**, **Labels**, **Data Labels** button and in the **More Data Label Options** section checked the **Category Name**, **Percentage** and **Show Leader Lines** check boxes. Then we just dragged things around and re-sized them.

This chart tells us, for example, that Wages for the whole year amount to 60% of the total yearly costs. Other cost categories are also displayed with their appropriate percentages. This chart is shown in full colour on the inside of the front cover of the book.

Saving a Chart as a Template

In Excel 2007 you can save your favourite chart designs as templates that you can reuse whenever you want. To do this, click the chart that you want to save as a template and click the **Design**, **Type**, **Save As Template** command button.

In the **Address Bar**, make sure that the Charts folder is selected, type a suitable name for the chart template in the **File name** box and click the **Save** button.

When you create a new chart or want to change the chart type of an existing chart, you can use your new chart template.

Fig. 6.14 Saving a Chart Template.

To create a new chart based on the template, click any chart type in the **Insert**, **Charts** group, and then click **All Chart Types**. Click **Templates** in the first **Charts Type** box, and then select the template that you want to use in the second box and click **OK**.

7

The Excel Database

An Excel database table is a worksheet range which contains related information, such as 'Customer's Name', 'Consultancy Details', 'Invoice No.', etc. A phone book is a simple database table, stored on paper. In Excel each record is entered as a worksheet row, with the fields of each record occupying corresponding columns.

A database table is a collection of data that exists, and is organised, around a specific theme or requirement. It is used for storing information so that it is quickly accessible. To make accessing the data easier, each row (or **record**), of data within a database table is structured in the same fashion, i.e. each record will have the same number of columns (or **fields**).

We define a database and its various elements as follows:

Database table   A collection of related data organised in rows and columns in a worksheet file which can contain many different database tables.

Record   A row of information relating to a single entry and comprising one or more fields.

Field   A single column of information of the same type, such as people's names.

Creating a Database

In order to investigate the various database functions, such as sorting, searching, etc., we first need to set up a database table in the form shown below.

Note that in creating a database table, the following rules must be observed:

1. The top row of the database table must contain the field labels, one per column, which identify the fields in the database table. The second and subsequent rows of such a database table must contain records; no blank rows should be inserted between the field labels and the records, or indeed anywhere between records.

2. Field labels must be unique within a given database table.

3. Entries under each field must be of the same type.

4. The size of a database table must be limited within the design criteria of the package.

We suggest that the 'Invoice Analysis' of Adept Consultants is designed and set out as shown below with the listed field titles and field widths.

Column	Title	Width	Type
A	NAME	21	General or Text
B	DETAILS	20	General or Text
C	No.	8	General or Text
D	ISSUED	11	Short Date, dd/mm/yy
E	PAID?	7	General or Text
F	VALUE	8	Currency, 2 decimals

These widths were chosen so that the whole worksheet could be seen on the screen at once, as shown in Fig. 7.1 on the next page.

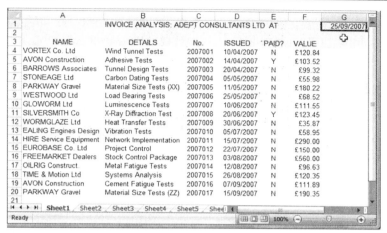

Fig. 7.1 A Set of Invoices for Adept Consultants.

If you cannot see all the rows of this database on your screen at once (it depends on the configuration of your

Fig. 7.2 Using the Zoom button to Set the Zoom level.

display under Windows), either select the **View** tab on the Ribbon, then click the **Zoom** icon in the **Zoom** group and set the **Custom** zoom level to say 90%, as shown in Fig. 7.2, or adjust the zoom level on the Zoom slide, shown here and located on the bottom right of the screen.

To change the width of the various columns to those given on the previous page, use the mouse to drag the vertical separators of the column borders. Next, enter the abbreviated titles, centrally positioned, in row 3, as shown in the worksheet above (Fig. 7.1).

The formatting type was selected by first clicking a column letter to select a whole column, then clicking the down-arrow in the **Number** group, shown in Fig. 7.3, and selecting the appropriate format style from the displayed drop-down list,.

Fig. 7.3 The Format Cells Dialogue Box.

This drop-down list was used to format columns A, B, C and E to a **General** category format, column D to a **Short Date** category format (type dd/mm/yy), and column F to a **Currency** format (with 2 decimal places).

Finally, enter the numeric information in your worksheet and save the worksheet under the filename **Invoice 1**. You could format your database further by freezing the range A1:G3, then clicking the **Home**, **Font**, **Fill Color** icon to shade the background of the selection to, say, a pale shade of blue. However, we leave this to you, as it is entirely a matter of personal choice.

Sorting a Database List

The records within our database list are in the order in which they were entered, with the invoice 'No.' shown in ascending order. However, we might find it easier to browse through the information if it was sorted in alphabetical order of customer's name. Excel has an easy way to do this.

To use it, highlight the database list (data range A4:F20; don't include the field names in the range to be sorted) and click the **Home**, **Editing**, **Sort & Filter** Ribbon icon and select the **Sort A to Z** option, shown here, which displays the sorted results shown in Fig. 7.4 below.

Fig. 7.4 The Sorted Invoices by Ascending Name.

Another method of sorting data, which allows more control over the sorting options, is to select the **Custom Sort** from the **Sort & Filter** list. This opens the Sort dialogue box displayed in Fig. 7.5, in which we show a composite of the available options for the **Sort by** fields and the **Sort On** items.

Fig. 7.5 The Sort Dialogue Box.

Note that in the **Sort On** list you can choose to sort your database on **Values**, **Cell Color**, **Font Color**, or **Cell Icon**. In the **Sort By** box you can choose the name of the field on which you want to sort the database (in this case NAME). This will be the primary sort key. Clicking the **Add Level** button pointed to in Fig. 7.6, adds another sort level, as shown below.

Fig. 7.6 A Two Level Sort.

The second sort level allows you additional control over the sorting options, by the selection of a secondary sort key (in this case No.) in the **Then by** list (see Fig. 7.5). In this case this ensures that the lowest number invoices appear first, if a company has been issued with more than one invoice. You even have the choice of a third sort key, if you needed one.

The easiest way to return the database to its original sort order is to re-sort it in ascending order of invoice No. However, for the time being leave it in alphabetical order.

Date Arithmetic

There are several date functions which can be used in Excel to carry out date calculations. For example, if the cell is formatted as **General**, typing the function =DATE(2007,9,25) returns the date 25/09/2007 and changes the format of the cell to 'Date'. The function =DATEVALUE("25/9/2007"), returns the date 25/09/2007 provided the cell is formatted as a **Date** category (type dd/mm/yy). If the cell in which you have typed such a function is formatted as **General** or **Number**, then Excel would return the number of days since 1 January 1900.

Typing the function =NOW( ), returns the current date and time as given by your computer's internal clock. The cell is formatted automatically as **General** (type dd/mm/yy hh.mm). If the cell was formatted as **Number**, then Excel would have returned a decimal number representing the number of days since 1 January 1900, with the digits after the decimal point representing a fraction of a day.

With Excel 2007 you don't need to use the DATE and DATEVALUE functions when entering dates. You could, for example, write in a cell the formula:

=NOW()−D4

This allows Excel to calculate the difference in days between now and the mentioned date, provided the cell was formatted as **Number**. We could use this formula to work out the number of overdue days of the unpaid invoices in our example, by typing it in cell G4. However, if you want to compare the numbers you get with those displayed in this book, use instead the following formula:

=$G$1−D4

where $G$1 causes an 'absolute' reference to be made to the contents of cell G1. If the record in row 4 refers to VORTEX Co. Ltd., then the result should be 168 days.

However, before we proceed to copy the above formula to the rest of the G column of the database list, we should take into consideration the fact that, normally, such information is not necessary if an invoice has been paid. Therefore, we need to edit the above formula in such a way as to make the result conditional to non-payment of the issued invoice.

The IF Function

The IF function allows comparison between two values using special 'logical' operators. The logical operators we can use are listed below.

Operator	*Meaning*
=	Equal to
<	Less than
>	Greater than
<=	Less than or Equal to
>=	Greater than or Equal to
<>	Not Equal to

The general format of the IF function is as follows:

IF(Comparison,Outcome-if-true,Outcome-if-false)

which contains three arguments separated by commas.

The first argument of the IF function is the 'logical comparison', the second is what should happen if the outcome of the logical comparison is 'true', while the third is what should happen if the outcome of the logical comparison is 'false'.

Thus, we can incorporate the IF function in the formula we entered in cell G4 to calculate the days overdue only if the invoice has not been paid, otherwise a blank string " " should be written into the appropriate cell, should the contents of the corresponding E column of a record be anything else but N. The final version of the formula in cell G4 should now correspond to:

=IF(E4="N",$G$1–D4," ")

Now copy this formula to the range (G5:G20) and compare your results with those shown in Fig. 7.7 below.

	A	B	C	D	E	F	G
1		INVOICE ANALYSIS: ADEPT CONSULTANTS LTD		AT			25/09/2007
2							
3	NAME	DETAILS	No.	ISSUED	PAID?	VALUE	OVERDUE
4	VORTEX Co. Ltd	Wind Tunnel Tests	2007001	10/04/2007	N	£120.84	168
5	AVON Construction	Adhesive Tests	2007002	14/04/2007	Y	£103.52	
6	BARROWS Associates	Tunnel Design Tests	2007003	20/04/2007	N	£99.32	158
7	STONEAGE Ltd	Carbon Dating Tests	2007004	05/05/2007	N	£55.98	143
8	PARKWAY Gravel	Material Size Tests (XX)	2007005	11/05/2007	N	£180.22	137
9	WESTWOOD Ltd	Load Bearing Tests	2007006	25/05/2007	N	£68.52	123
10	GLOWORM Ltd	Luminescence Tests	2007007	10/06/2007	N	£111.55	107
11	SILVERSMITH Co	X-Ray Diffraction Test	2007008	20/06/2007	Y	£123.45	
12	WORMGLAZE Ltd	Heat Transfer Tests	2007009	30/06/2007	N	£35.87	87
13	EALING Engines Design	Vibration Tests	2007010	05/07/2007	N	£58.95	82
14	HIRE Service Equipment	Network Implementation	2007011	15/07/2007	N	£290.00	72
15	EUROBASE Co. Ltd	Project Control	2007012	22/07/2007	N	£150.00	65
16	FREEMARKET Dealers	Stock Control Package	2007013	03/08/2007	N	£560.00	53
17	OILRIG Construct.	Metal Fatigue Tests	2007014	12/08/2007	N	£96.63	44
18	TIME & Motion Ltd	Systems Analysis	2007015	26/08/2007	N	£120.35	30
19	AVON Construction	Cement Fatigue Tests	2007016	07/09/2007	N	£111.89	18
20	PARKWAY Gravel	Material Size Tests (ZZ)	2007017	15/09/2007	N	£190.35	10
21							

Sheet1 / Sheet2 / Sheet3 / Sheet4 / Sheet5 / Shee

Ready 100%

Fig. 7.7 Demonstrating the Use of the IF Function in the Overdue Column.

Your results might differ from the ones shown above, if you have used the NOW( ) function in cell G1. Check your work, then save it under the file name **Invoice 2**.

Conditional Formatting

New to Excel 2007 is the ability to format cells according to certain conditions. The idea for this type of formatting is that normally it is very difficult to see patterns and trends in large data by just looking at numbers.

Referring to our small invoicing example, it is rather difficult to see at a glance which companies are behind with their payments by just looking at the numbers in the 'Overdue' column, particularly if the database has been sorted in alphabetical order of company 'Name'.

In Fig. 7.8 on the next page, we show how conditional formatting works. First, select the data you want to conditionally format; in our case cell range G4:G20. Then, on the **Home** tab click the **Conditional Formatting** button in the **Styles** group and select the **Data Bars** option from the displayed menu. We then chose the **Purple Data Bar** pointed to in Fig. 7.8. Note that as the mouse pointer hovers over the other bars, the data in the selected range changes colour. As you can see it is now very easy to identify the long overdue invoices.

In Fig. 7.9, also on the next page, we show the effect of choosing the **Red to Black** from the **Icon Sets** option. This is shown together with the **Purple Data Bar** formatting, but you can choose to remove the latter by selecting the **Clear Rules** option before selecting to mark your data with an icon set.

To find out more on this subject, search Excel Help for **Conditional Formatting** and have a look at the Demo.

Fig. 7.8 Using Conditional Formatting with Data Bars.

Fig. 7.9 Using Conditional Formatting with Data Bars and Icon Sets.

Now save your work again under the filename **Invoice 2** before going on.

Managing Conditional Rules

Assuming that the database **Invoice 2** is on your screen, we will first remove the conditional formatting we had imposed on it so far. To do this, select the range G4:G20, then click the **Home**, **Styles**, **Conditional Formatting** button and select **Clear Rules**, then **Clear Rules from Selected Cells**, as shown in Fig. 7.10 below.

Fig. 7.10 Clearing Conditional Formatting.

Next, and with the same range selected, click the **Conditional Formatting** button, but this time select the **New Rules** option from the drop-down menu which opens the **New Formatting Rule** window, the lower part of which is shown in Fig. 7.11 on the next page, having accepted the default **Format all cells based on their values** on the upper part of the screen.

Fig. 7.11 The New Formatting Rule Screen (Lower Part).

We now need to go through a procedure outlined below before we can start querying the database.

- Click the down-arrow against the **Format Style** box and select **Icon Sets** from the drop-down menu pointed to in Fig. 7.11 above which changes the lower part of the screen, as shown in Fig. 7.12, to accommodate our new requirements.

Fig. 7.12 The Changed Lower Part of the New Formatting Rule Screen.

- On the changed screen, click the down-arrow against **Percent** and change both the **Type** values from the default to **Number** by choosing from the displayed drop-down menu.

The moment the **Type** is changed to **Number** the corresponding default numerical values of 67 and 33 disappear from their respective places on the window and you can enter your own numbers as follows:

- Click the button at the far right of the first **Value** box to open the screen below.

- Type, say, 90 and click the button to the right of the box pointed to above. This causes the number you typed to be entered in the **New Formatting Rule** window.

- Repeat the above procedure but enter 60 in the displayed box.

- Click the down-arrow against the **Icon Style** box and select the **3 Symbols (Uncircled)** option from the drop-down menu.

- Check the **Reverse Icon Order** box, so that now the red cross ✖ icon represents **Number** values greater or equal to 90, the yellow exclamation mark ❗ represents values less than 90 but greater or equal to 60, and the green check mark ✔ represents values less than 60.

The final **New Formatting Rule** screen should look like the one shown in Fig. 7.13 on the next page.

Note: The numeric values of 60 and 30 were chosen randomly as an example. You, of course, could type your own values to reflect your specific needs. Explaining this procedure takes a lot longer than executing it, so don't be put off!

Fig. 7.13 The Final New Formatting Rule Screen (Lower Part).

Finally, click **OK** and on the reopened **Conditional Formatting Rules Manager** screen click **Apply** to see the icons appear on the selected range of cells and, if satisfied, click **OK** to fix them in place. Your screen should now look similar to ours below (Fig. 7.14).

Fig. 7.14 The Excel Screen Showing 3 Conditional Symbols.

Finally, to visually enhance the 'Overdue' column, add the **Purple Data Bar** option to it from the **Data Bars** list (see page 108), and save your work as **Invoice 3**.

Searching a Database

We will use the enhanced database of **Invoice 3** to find records with overdue payment. To see the database in full colour, have a look inside the back cover of the book where we also show the results of filtered records.

Filtering Records

Excel 2007 has a new, very easy, way of finding specific records from within a database involving conditional formatting, whether this is by cell colour or by cell symbols (or icons).

To start the process, select the data range which you have formatted conditionally, in our example this is G3:G20, as shown in Fig. 7.15. Note that we have included the heading 'Overdue' in the selected range.

Fig. 7.15 Preparing to Filter Records.

Next, click the **Home**, **Editing**, **Sort & Filter** button, and select **Filter** from the drop-down menu also shown in Fig. 7.15. Doing so, places a down-arrow button on the right of the cell 'Overdue', as shown in Fig. 7.16 on the next page. Clicking this down-arrow, displays a sub-menu, also shown in Fig. 7.16 on the next page.

Fig. 7.16 Selecting a Filter.

As you can see, you can either use **Number Filters**, in which case you'll have to provide the filter criteria, or **Filter by Color**. Choosing the latter displays a further sub-menu which lists the coloured cell icons you used to conditionally format your selected data range.

If you click the red cross symbol, pointed to above, Excel displays only the data marked with this symbol, as shown in Fig. 7.17 below.

Fig. 7.17 Filtered Data by Symbol.

To remove the filter, click the **Clear** option from the drop-down menu shown above. To filter the data with another symbol click the down-arrow in the 'Overdue' cell. To see filtered data in colour, have a look at the inside of the back cover of the book.

Finding Records

To find records that include specified text, conditional formatting or formulae, use the **Home**, **Editing**, **Find & Select** button, as shown in Fig. 7.18 below.

Fig. 7.18 Finding Records with Formulae or Conditional Formatting.

It so happens that in our example the range G4:G20 is the only range that contains both conditional formatting and formulae, so the same range is highlighted when we select either of these two options from the drop-down menu shown above.

To find records that contain specified text, choose the **Find** option from the above drop-down menu. This opens the Find and Replace dialogue box in which you type the text you are looking for in your data, then clicking the **Find All** button displays the ranges of the records containing the specified text at the bottom of the dialogue box, and highlights the first such record in the database.

In Fig. 7.19 below, we display a composite showing what we typed in the Find and Replace dialogue box ('Control' in our example) and the result of the **Find All** action.

Fig. 7.19 Finding Records Containing Specified Text.

Filtering and Removing Duplicate Records

Filtering for unique values and removing duplicate values are closely related operations which display the same results. However, there is a major difference – filtering for unique values only temporarily hides duplicate values, while removing duplicate values permanently deletes such values.

It is, therefore, a good idea to filter for unique values first before permanently removing duplicate values from a database, to confirm that indeed that is what you are intending all along.

To filter for unique values, we need to specify an area of the worksheet for setting our criteria for the search. To do this, first copy the field names of the database (A3:G3) to an empty area of the worksheet, say, A23:G23 which will form the first line of the 'criteria range'. Label this area CRITERIA FOR SEARCHING in cell A22.

Now type in cells E24 and F24 the actual criteria (N and >150), respectively, then click the **Data**, **Sort & Filter**, **Advanced** button pointed to in Fig. 7.20, and specify in the displayed dialogue box the **List range** and **Criteria range** as $A$3:$G$20 and $A$23:$G$24 (it includes the field names in both cases). Pressing the **OK** button, causes Excel to **Filter the list, in-place** by hiding the rows that do not meet the criteria, as shown below.

Fig. 7.20 Using the Data, Advanced Filter to Search a Database.

The above screen dump is a composite – it shows what action you have to take and the result of that action. To return your display to the full database list, click the **Data**, **Sort & Filter**, **Clear** button.

Note: Do not specify an empty line as part of the criterion range, as this has the effect of searching the database for **all** records.

The criteria must be entered in the second and subsequent rows of the criterion range, with each entered below the copy of the appropriate field name. A label (text) or a value may be entered exactly as it appears in the database.

In the case of searching a database for label (text), such as under the fields 'NAME' and 'DETAILS' in our example, you can use the two special characters ? and * (known as 'wildcard characters') to match any single character of a label or all characters to the end of the label, as shown in Fig. 7.21.

Fig. 7.21 Using Wildcard Characters in a Search.

To search a database for values, either enter the value as the exact criterion or use a simple numeric comparison, such as >90, in which the logical operators (<, <=, >, >=, <>) can be used. The logical formula generates a value of 1 if the condition is TRUE or a value of 0 if the condition is FALSE.

Several criteria can be entered, either in the same row, or one per row. You choose the former if you want Excel to search for records that match every criterion (i.e. criteria entered are linked with the logical AND), or the latter, if you want Excel to search records that satisfy any of the criteria (i.e. criteria entered are linked with the logical OR). You can also choose a combination of the two, as shown in Fig. 7.22 on the next page. Remember to increase the criteria range to accommodate the extra row.

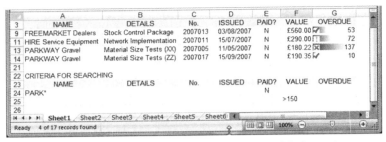

Fig. 7.22 Demonstrating the Logical AND and OR Operators.

Finally, don't forget to click the **Data, Sort & Filter**, **Clear** button to display the full database list before re-specifying your data and criteria ranges each time you embark on a new search.

To remove duplicate records, first filter them using the method discussed above, but with the criteria given below.

	A	B	C	D	E	F	G
3	NAME	DETAILS	No.	ISSUED	PAID?	VALUE	OVERDUE
4	AVON Construction	Adhesive Tests	2007002	14/04/2007	Y	£103.52	
5	AVON Construction	Cement Fatigue Tests	2007016	07/09/2007	N	£111.89	18
13	PARKWAY Gravel	Material Size Tests (XX)	2007005	11/05/2007	N	£180.22	137
14	PARKWAY Gravel	Material Size Tests (ZZ)	2007017	15/09/2007	N	£190.35	10
21							
22	CRITERIA FOR SEARCHING						
23	NAME	DETAILS	No.	ISSUED	PAID?	VALUE	OVERDUE
24	PARK*						
25	AVON *						
26							

Ready   4 of 17 records found   100%

Fig. 7.23 Searching for Duplicates with the Logical OR Operator.

If these are the duplicate records found and you want to remove one of each, then click the **Data**, **Data Tools**, **Remove Duplicates** button, and in the displayed dialogue box select the NAME as the only column for the search criteria. Clicking the **OK** button, removes all duplicates from the database – one AVON and one PARKWAY. Try it, then click the **Undo** button to recover the original database.

Extracting Records

To extract records and have them copied into another area of the worksheet, we need to select the **Copy to another location** option in the Advanced Filter dialogue box. But first, we need to set up a second area – the 'output range'. To do this, copy the field names to the cell range $A$28:$G$28 and label it as 'OUTPUT RANGE' in cell A27, as shown in Fig. 7.24 below.

Fig. 7.24 Extracting Data into an Output Range.

The above screen dump is a composite – it shows what action you have to take and the result of that action.

Note that in our example we have chosen to put the criteria and output ranges in rows below the actual database (perhaps not the best position), rather than on the side of it. This avoids the errors that might ensue should we later decide to insert a row in our database, which will also insert a row in the criteria/output range. For a more structured worksheet layout, see below.

Finally, save the worksheet under the filename **Invoice 4**, before going on.

Structuring a Workbook

In a well designed workbook, areas of calculations using formulae should be kept on a separate sheet from the data entry sheet. The reason for this is to prevent accidental overwriting of formulae that might be contained within the data entry sheet.

As an example, we will use the **Invoice 4** file, but instead of extracting data into the same sheet, we will use another sheet into which to copy the extracted records. To do this, first open file **Invoice 4**, then click the **View**, **Window**, **New Window** button, followed by the **Arrange All** button and in the displayed Arrange Windows dialogue box click the **Horizontal** radio button and click **OK**.

Next, activate the lower window and click on the Sheet2 tab to display an empty worksheet at the bottom half of the screen, as shown in Fig. 7.25 on the next page.

Fig. 7.25 Structuring a Workbook.

Now use the **Cut** (Ctrl+X) and **Paste** (Ctrl+V) commands to transfer cell range A22:G28 of Sheet1 to a range starting at cell A1 of Sheet2 and adjust the widths of the various columns to match those of Sheet1 (also, don't forget to delete from Sheet1 any extracted data from a previous search).

The address in the **List range** box of the Advanced Filter dialogue box must be specified (you can either type it in or use the buttons to the right of the entry box to point to the required range) to indicate the correct address for the database list which is

Sheet1!$A$3:$G$20

Note: Excel only extracts data into an active sheet. Therefore, you must make Sheet2 the active sheet and since the program also requires to know which are the database field labels, place the cell pointer in cell A7, before you use the **Data, Sort & Filter, Advanced** command.

The **Criteria range** and the **Copy to** address locations should be similarly prefixed with Sheet2 for correct data extraction. To access the entry box of the latter, click the **Copy to another location** radio button on the Advanced Filter dialogue box, as shown in Fig. 7.26.

Fig. 7.26 Preparing to Extract Data into Another Location.

Pressing the **OK** button causes the records that match the specified criteria to be extracted from Sheet1 and copied into Sheet2, as shown in Fig. 7.27 below.

	A	B	C	D	E	F	G
1	CRITERIA FOR SEARCHING						
2	NAME	DETAILS	No.	ISSUED	PAID?	VALUE	OVERDUE
3	PARK*				N		
4						>150	
5							
6	OUTPUT RANGE						
7	NAME	DETAILS	No.	ISSUED	PAID?	VALUE	OVERDUE
8	FREEMARKET Dealers	Stock Control Package	2007013	03/08/2007	N	£560.00	53
9	HIRE Service Equipment	Network Implementation	2007011	15/07/2007	N	£290.00	72
10	PARKWAY Gravel	Material Size Tests (XX)	2007005	11/05/2007	N	£180.22	137
11	PARKWAY Gravel	Material Size Tests (ZZ)	2007017	15/09/2007	N	£190.35	10
12							

Fig. 7.27 Extracted Data into Sheet2 of Workbook.

Save the workbook under the file name **Invoice 5**.

Another aspect of structuring is the provision of a screen with technical information about the contents of the particular workbook; a kind of overview of the function of the worksheet application. This area should also contain instructions for the use of the particular application at hand. Such information can help you in the future, or help others to learn and use an application easily and effectively. If you use range names, then include a range name table in your information screen(s).

Finally, provide a separate sheet within a workbook, or a separate worksheet altogether, for macros (discussed in Chapter 10), which are in a programming language that allows you to chain together commands. Sensitive sheets or indeed whole workbooks can be protected using the **Review** tab, then clicking either the **Protect Sheet** or the **Protect Workbook** button in the **Changes** group, according to your application needs, to restrict cell entries to unprotected cells. This prevents accidental changes being made to cells containing formulae.

A good spreadsheet design, using the 3-dimensional ability of Excel could be as shown in Fig. 7.28 below.

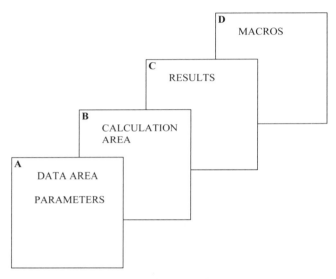

Fig. 7.28 A Suggested Structure for a Workbook.

Obviously, the headings of the various workbook sheets above could be different. They would largely depend on the application at hand.

8

Other Tools and Capabilities

As well as the **Spelling** and **Thesaurus** tools, to be found under the **Proofing** group of the **Review** tab of the Ribbon, Excel includes a **Formula Auditing** capability (to be found in the **Formulas** tab) and tools to carry out What-If Analysis (to be found in the **Data** tab), used to solve problems such as the **Goal Seek**, **Data Tables**, and **Scenarios**. A short description of each of these is given below.

Formula Auditing

You use the Formula Auditing capability of Excel to analyse the way your worksheet is structured, or for locating the source of errors in formulae. You will find everything you need in the **Formula Auditing** group of the **Formulas** tab of the Ribbon, as shown in Fig. 8.1.

Fig. 8.1 The Formula Auditing Group.

In this you can specify what you want to audit on the current file. For a description of the options see next page.

The Formula Auditing options have the following functions:

Option	*Function*
Trace Precedents	Identifies with arrows all cells that affect the currently selected cell.
Trace Dependents	Identifies with arrows all cells that are affected by the value of the currently selected cell.
Remove Arrows	Removes the identifying arrows placed on the worksheet as a result of invoking the previous options.
Show Formulas	Displays the actual formulae you have entered in cells with their effective range of their arguments marked in blue outline.
Error Checking	Identifies all cells involved in the production of an error, such as a circular reference.
Evaluate Formula	Launches the Evaluation Formula dialogue box to debug a formula by evaluating each part of the formula in the selected cell.
Watch Window	Watch cells and their formulae on the Watch Window, as changes are made to the worksheet even when the cells are out of view.

As an example, in Fig. 8.2 we show an audit on the file **Project 3**, for the first two options. For the first option, select cell E11, then click the **Formulas**, **Formula Auditing**, **Trace Precedents** button, while for the second option, select cell B12, then click the **Trace Dependents** button.

Fig. 8.2 Illustrating the Trace Precedents and Trace Dependents Options.

To remove the arrows resulting from the above choice of auditing options, click the **Remove Arrows** button, then click the **Show Formulas** command button to display Fig. 8.3.

	A	B	C	D	E
1	*Project Analysis:*				
2					
3		Jan	Feb	Mar	1st Quarter
4	Income	14000	15000	16000	=SUM(B4:D4)
5	Costs:				
6	Wages	2000	3000	4000	=SUM(B6:D6)
7	Travel	400	500	600	=SUM(B7:D7)
8	Rent	300	300	300	=SUM(B8:D8)
9	Heat/Light	150	200	130	=SUM(B9:D9)
10	Phone/Fax	250	300	350	=SUM(B10:D10)
11	Adverts	1100	1200	1300	=SUM(B11:D11)
12	Total Costs	=SUM(B6:B11)	=SUM(C6:C11)	=SUM(D6:D11)	=SUM(B12:D12)
13	Profit	=B4-B12	=C4-C12	=D4-D12	=E4-E12
14	Cumulative	=B13	=B14+C13	=C14+D13	
15					

Fig. 8.3 Illustrating the Show Formulas Option.

To return to normal viewing, click the **Show Formulas** button again – it acts as a toggle switch.

As an example of evaluating a formula step by step, select cell D14 then click the **Formulas**, **Formula Auditing**, **Evaluate Formula** button to open the Evaluate Formula dialogue box displaying the formula C14+D13 with the first section of the formula underlined. Clicking the **Evaluate** button at the bottom of the dialogue box displays its value and moves the underline to the next section of the formula, as shown in Fig. 8.4 below.

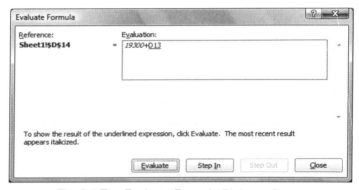

Fig. 8.4 The Evaluate Formula Dialogue Box.

Clicking the **Evaluate** button again, displays the value of the second section of the formula and underlines the two displayed values. Clicking the **Evaluate** button yet again, displays the result that is also shown in cell D14 in the worksheet. Clicking the **Evaluate** button once more, starts the process all over again.

The Watch Window

The adoption of the Watch Window allows the calculated values of specified cells to be displayed in a window as you work so that you can see the results even if you are working on another, faraway part of the worksheet or workbook.

In the composite display in Fig. 8.5 below, we have first selected cells E11, E12, and E13 of the **Project 3** file, then clicked the **Formulas**, **Formula Auditing**, **Watch Window** button. This opens a floating Watch Window, and clicking the **Add Watch** button opens the Add Watch box displaying the range of the selected worksheet cells. Clicking the **Add** button, transfers this selection from the Add Watch box to the Watch Window which now remains visible on screen even when you select another worksheet.

Fig. 8.5 Illustrating the Use of the Watch Window.

You can remove individual parts of what you were watching, by clicking their entry in the Watch Window dialogue box and then clicking the **Delete Watch** button which is situated on the same dialogue box and to the right of the **Add Watch** button. To remove all watched items at once, click the **Formulas**, **Formula Auditing**, **Watch Window** button again – it acts as a toggle switch.

What-If Analysis

Excel allows you to create and manage Scenarios for What-If Analysis. A scenario is a set of values that Excel saves and can substitute automatically on your worksheet. You can use scenarios to forecast the outcome of a worksheet model.

Creating a Scenario

We will use **Project 3** to find out what the effect on 'Cumulative' profits of the first quarter of Adept Consultants would be if the 'Wages' in the month of January were increased (a) to the level of February, and (b) to the level of March.

To start, select cell B6 then click the **Data**, **Data Tools**, **What-If Analysis** button and select the **Scenario Manager** from the drop-down list. Next, click the **Add** button on the displayed Scenario Manager dialogue box to open the **Add Scenario** box, in which we gave the name of our first scenario as 'Equal to Feb', and in the next box we entered the value of 3000, then repeated the

process and gave the name to our second scenario as 'Equal to Mar' and gave it a value of 4000. The resulting Scenario Manager dialogue box is shown in Fig. 8.6.

Fig. 8.6 Illustrating the Scenario Manager.

Next, click the **Summary** button and in the Scenario Summary box change what is displayed in the **Result cell** box by selecting cell D14 on your worksheet and clicking **OK**. The Scenario Summary sheet is then displayed as shown below.

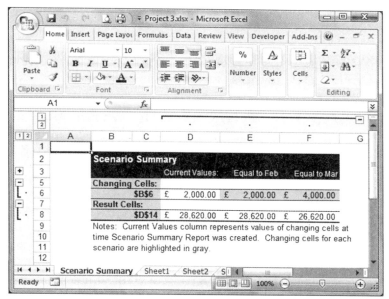

Fig. 8.7 The Scenario Summary Sheet.

Excel displays all three results; 'Current Values', 'Equal to Feb', and 'Equal to Mar' for you to compare at a glance. Save this workbook under the filename **Tools 1**.

If you wanted to remove the Scenario Summary sheet from your workbook, and start again, click the **Home**, **Cells**, **Delete** button and select **Delete Sheet** from the drop-down list.

The Goal Seek

You use **Goal Seek** to fine-tune a formula that gives you the required result by changing one of the variables that affect the final value. As an example, we will use the information in the **Tools 1** file. If you don't have this file, use the **Project 3** file.

To effectively use Goal Seek, first type the formula to be fine-tuned by Excel in a cell. We will use the **=sum(B4:D4)** formula in cell E4 of **Sheet1** of our example.

Next, click the **Data**, **Data Tools**, **What-If Analysis** button and select **Goal Seek** from the drop-down menu to display the Goal Seek dialogue box shown in Fig. 8.8 below.

Fig. 8.8 Using the Goal Seek.

In this dialogue box you can specify in the **Set cell** box the address or range name of the cell that contains the formula you want to fine-tune, E4 in our example. In the **To value** box you type the value you want the formula in the formula cell to equate to when Goal Seek solves the problem, 40000 in our example, while in the **By changing cell** box you type the address of the cell whose value Goal Seek can change, $B$4 in our example.

Click the **OK** button to find an answer to the problem, displayed in Fig. 8.9 on the next page – it changed the contents of B4 from £14,000 to £9,000. If it can't be done, you will be informed.

Fig. 8.9 Goal Seek Finding a Solution.

If you don't want to lose the original values in the adjustable cell, then press the **Cancel** button.

What-if Data Tables

What-if data tables are used if you require to calculate and display the results of substituting different values for one or more (up to three) variables in a formula.

For example, suppose we wanted to examine the effect to the quarterly profits of Adept Consultants if we varied the quarterly income from £35,000 to £55,000, in steps of £5,000. This problem is rather trivial, but suppose at the same time we expected a wage award increase of between 0% to 3%, while all other costs were tied to inflation which could change from 3% to 5%. This becomes rather more difficult to analyse. However, using what-if tables reduces the problem to something more manageable.

A Two-Input What-if Data Table

To illustrate the above problem, but simplifying it by forgetting inflation, we will use the **Tools 1** file. First select cell A4 and click the **View**, **Window, Freeze Panes** button, and select the **Freeze First Column** option, then fill in the range F2:K9, as shown below in Fig. 8.10 and save the result as **Tools 2**.

Fig. 8.10 Designing a Two-Input What-if Data Table.

Note: A two-input what-if data table has two input cells – in our example these are: Input 1 in cell G2 (which refers to the rows) and input 2 in cell G3 (which refers to the columns), representing 'Wage increases' and 'Income', respectively. The value in each of these cells is the first value in their respective ranges, which are F6:F9 and G5:K5. Thus, income varies from £35,000 to £55,000, while wage increases vary from 0% to 3%.

Finally, a formula is required in cell F5 which represents profits and which refers to the two input cells defined above. The formula used is:

   =G3-(E6*(1+G2)+SUM(E7:E11))

To verify that this formula is correct, change the input in the 'Income' cell (G3) to £45,000, which should give you the same profit in cell F5 as that shown in cell E13.

The formula in a two-input what-if table must be placed in the top-left corner of the table. Which cell is declared as a 'row input' and a 'column input' in the Table dialogue box is very important.

In the case of a one-input what-if table, Excel expects the input range to be either in one column, with the formula placed in the row above the first value and one cell to the right of the input range, or in one row, with the formula placed in the column to the left of the first value and one cell below the row of the input range.

Before going on, save your work under the filename **Tools 2**, then select the effective table range F5:K9. Next, click the **Data**, **Data Tools**, **What-If Analysis** button, select the **Data Table** option and enter $G$3 in the **Row input cell** box of the displayed dialogue box, and $G$2 in the **Column input Cell** box as shown in Fig. 8.11.

Fig. 8.11 Allocating Parameters to a Two-Input What-if Table.

Pressing the **OK** button displays the results shown in Fig. 8.12 below. You could now save this example under the file name **Tools 3**.

Fig. 8.12 The Results of a Two-Input What-if Data Table.

Editing a Data Table

The input values and formula in the top leftmost column of a data table can be edited at any time. However, the actual results calculated within the data table cannot be edited individually, because they are an array. Some editing operations require you to select the entire data table, while others require you to select only the resulting values. For example:

- To clear the resulting values from a data table, select the resulting values only (G6:K9 in our example) and press the **Del** key. Individual resulting values cannot be cleared separately.

- To copy resulting values from a data table, select them and use the **Copy** (**Ctrl+C**) command. Doing this results in copying the values only, not the formulae for those values.

Subsequent use of the **Paste Special** command converts the resulting values array into a range of constant values.

- To move, delete, or modify a table, first select the entire data table (F5:K9 in our example). If you are moving the table, having selected it, then click the border of the selection and drag it to a new location on your worksheet.

The Solver

You use the Solver if you want to analyse data in a worksheet and solve 'what-if' type problems. Solver is ideal for problems that have more than one answer. It can investigate different options and present you with alternative solutions, including the best match to your requirements.

Before you can use the Solver, you might need to install it, as it is an add-in and it might not have been

installed automatically by **Setup** – you will know if it is installed already as its name will then appear on the **Data** tab of the Ribbon in the **Analysis** group. If it does not, you will need to install it by clicking the **Microsoft Office Button**, then the **Excel Options** pointed to in Fig. 8.13.

Fig. 8.13 The Excel Options Button.

In the displayed Excel Options dialogue box, click the **Add-Ins** button in the left pane, select Excel Add-ins in the Manage box at the bottom of the dialogue box and click **Go**. In the Add-Ins available box, select the **Solver Add-in** check box, and then click **OK**. The program will then automatically install it for you.

Fig. 8.14 The Add-Ins in the Excel Options Dialogue Box.

In Fig. 8.14 above, we show what you have to do and the result of that action.

To use the Solver option, you start with a worksheet model. Solver problems can be set up in one or more worksheet files in memory, by selecting which cells to adjust, adding logical formulae and defining the limits of the required answers.

As an example, let us analyse more closely Adept Consultants' 1st Quarter results. We use the information held in Sheet1 of the **Tools 1** file.

On Sheet2 of the file, add the text and equations shown in Fig. 8.15 below and save the resultant workbook under the file name **Tools 4**.

Fig. 8.15 The Solver Exercise Entered in Sheet2 of the Workbook.

What we assume in this exercise is that Adept Consultants operate both at home and abroad. In the first quarter they undertook 30 consultancies at home and 20 consultancies abroad. We also assume that the income per consultancy for 'Home' to be equal to 2/3 of the total income for the 1st quarter, while the income per consultancy for 'Abroad' to be equal to 1/3 of the total income for the 1st quarter.

Similarly the costs per consultancy for 'Home' and 'Abroad' are assumed to be in the same ratio as those for the income. However, the time spent (hours per consultancy) are set for 'Home' and 'Abroad' to be 60 and 160 respectively, because of extra travelling time.

In the range C10:D14 of the worksheet we proceed to work out the 'Total Profit' in terms of 'Profit per hour'. The reason for this is that later in this chapter we will examine what happens to profit/hour if the hours taken to complete a consultancy were to be varied.

Below we show the actual values that should appear in the worksheet if all formulae are entered correctly. The values in column E either summate the two types of consultancies or contain crosschecks of our workings.

Cells E13 and E14 hold the total time spent in consultancies and the total profit made, respectively, which is very important information.

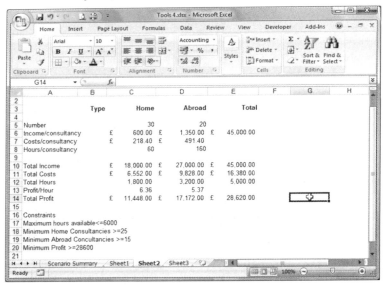

Fig. 8.16 The Solver Exercise Entered in Sheet2 of the Workbook.

What we would like to do now is to increase the consultancies to make up the maximum available time in the three month period, which is 6000 hours, while maximising the profit. The question is 'what mixture of consultancies (home or abroad) is more profitable?'

Starting the Solver

To start Solver click the **Data**, **Analysis**, **Solver** button, which displays the Solver Parameters dialogue box shown in Fig. 8.17.

Fig. 8.17 The Solver Parameters Box.

Next, we enter the constraints under which we will impose a solution to our problem. These can be added, changed or deleted using the three buttons at the bottom of the Solver Parameters dialogue box.

Entering Constraints

At the bottom of the worksheet we have included certain constraints, discussed below. These are entered as logical formulae using the Add Constraint dialogue box, shown in Fig. 8.18 below, opened by clicking the **Add** button on the Solver Parameters dialogue box to enter the first constraint. Then by clicking the **Add** button on the Add Constraint box to add subsequent constraints.

Fig. 8.18 The Add Constraint Box.

The logic behind these constraints is as follows:

- Since the maximum available hours in a quarter must remain less than or equal to 6000, we enter as the first constraint the formula **\$E\$12<=6000**.

- Since a long-term contract with the government requires that at least 25 consultancies are undertaken at home, we enter as the second constraint the formula **\$C\$5>=25**.

- Since a similar long-term contract with a foreign government requires that at least 15 consultancies are undertaken abroad, we enter as the third constraint the formula **\$D\$5>=15**.

Solving a Problem

Once the last constraint is inserted into the Add Constraint dialogue box, clicking the **OK** button opens the Solver Preferences box, shown in Fig. 8.19 below.

Fig. 8.19 The Solver Preferences Box.

Next, specify the **Set Target Cell** as \$E\$14, then the adjustable cells in the **By Changing Cells** box as \$C\$5:\$D\$5 – these are cells that contain values that Solver can adjust when it searches for an answer.

Finally, click the **Solve** button and let Solver find a solution, place the answer in the worksheet and display the Solver Results dialogue box, as shown in Fig. 8.20.

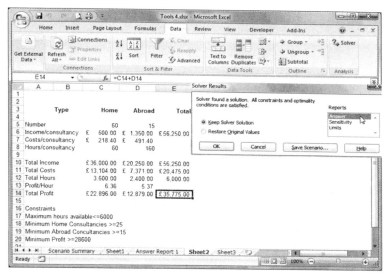

Fig. 8.20 The Solver Results.

You now have a choice of either keeping the values found by Solver or reverting to the original worksheet values. Also from the **Reports** section of the dialogue box you can choose to display one of three report types: Answer, Sensitivity, and Limits. Selecting one of these causes Excel to produce an appropriate report and place it in a separate Sheet. In Fig. 8.21 on the next page, we show the results for an Answer Report.

Note: Excel does not always produce an Answer Report as easily as that. Instead, on a number of occasions we received a warning message telling us that Excel encountered an internal error or that we ran out of memory even though our PC has 2 GB of RAM!

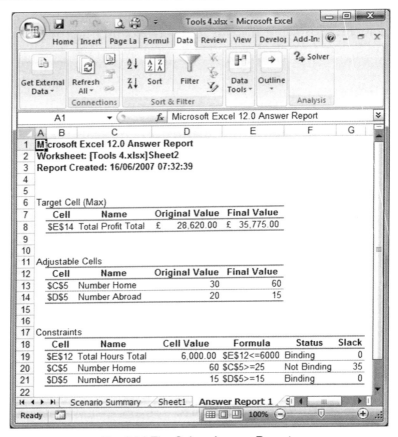

Fig. 8.21 The Solver Answer Report.

Finally, save your work under the filename **Tools 5**.

If a problem is too complex for the default settings of Solver, then click the **Options** button on the Solver Parameters dialogue box to display the Solver Options dialogue box, in which you can change the time limit for solving a problem, the maximum iterations allowed, and even select the type of model to be used.

Managing What-if Scenarios

There may be times when we would like to examine different what-if scenarios created from a single spreadsheet model. Normally, managers tend to copy the model to different parts of the spreadsheet so as to examine and display different assumptions. However, keeping track of all the different assumptions can become extremely problematic, confusing, and indeed wasteful of spreadsheet space and computer memory.

With Excel you can use the Scenario Manager to keep all the different versions of the same worksheet model together. In addition you can also give each version a meaningful name, such as 'Original Case', 'Best Case', and 'Worst Case'.

We will use the **Tools 5** example to illustrate the method. In addition, we assume that it is possible to reduce the number of hours it takes Adept Consultants to complete a consultancy at home or abroad, but if one is reduced the other is increased by the same amount.

The model looks as shown in Fig. 8.22 on the next page, with '% Changes' added in columns F and G, the contents of cells C8 and D8 changed to =60*(1+F8) and =160*(1+G8) respectively, and the overall profit now also displayed in column H, by inserting in H5 the reference =E14. Obviously, since we will be optimising our solutions, you must learn to use Solver first.

Next, enter 0% change in the hours per consultancy on both the home and abroad input cells, which reflects the 'Original' state of our problem with an optimum answer on profits using the already defined constraints. This gives a profit of £35,775 – the no-change scenario.

Fig. 8.22 Designing a What-if Scenarios Worksheet.

Finally, save your model as **Tools 6** before going on. This ensures that you can go back to it if anything goes wrong when trying to run the **Scenarios** option.

Next, click the **Data**, **Data Tools**, **What-If Analysis**, **Scenarios** icon and select **Scenario Manager** from the drop-down menu to open its dialogue box which, at this point, contains no scenarios. To start the process, press

the **Add** button to display the Add Scenario dialogue box shown in Fig. 8.23. Now add the description 'Original Version' in the **Scenario name** text box, then specify in the **Changing cells** F8:G8.

Fig. 8.23 The Add Scenario Box.

Pressing the **OK** button, displays the Scenario Values dialogue box, shown in Fig. 8.24, with the values for both F8 and G8 showing as 0 (zero). Pressing the **OK** button

returns you to the Scenario Manager dialogue box with the recently created scenario appearing in the **Scenarios** list box.

Fig. 8.24 The Scenario Values Box.

Next, repeat the process by pressing the **Add** button on the Scenario Manager dialogue box to display the Add Scenario dialogue box in which you type a name for the second scenario, say 'Negative Home Change'. Then, change the values for cells F8 and G8 to –5% and 5%, respectively, in the Scenario Values dialogue box (the actual values should be entered as -0.05 and 0.05).

Finally, repeat the process to create a 'Positive Home Change' with Scenario Values in F8 and G8 of 5% and –5%, respectively.

To see and select any one of the defined scenarios, use the Scenario Manager dialogue box, shown in Fig. 8.25 on the next page (activated by the **Data**, **Data Tools**, **What-If Analysis**, **Scenario Manager**), with all the different versions of the solutions listed. To look at the results of one of these, simply highlight it and press the **Show** button. The only changes you'll see are those relating to hours spent consulting and profits per hour.

Finally, save your work under the file name **Tools 7**. In this way you always have **Tools 6** to revert to in case any errors occur in the final version of our example.

Fig. 8.25 Using The Scenario Manager to View Different Scenarios.

Last but not least, Scenario Manager allows you to merge several versions together and define them as a scenario, and also create a summary report – you have a choice of two. The first report is a 'scenario summary', while the second is a 'scenario pivot table'. With the pivot table you get an instant what-if analysis of different scenario combinations, as shown in Fig. 8.26.

Fig. 8.26 The Scenario Pivot Table.

9

Sharing Information

Office 2007 is the most integrated suite to come from the Microsoft stables. The new **Themes** feature makes it easy to keep consistent colours, fonts, and special effects between Excel 2007, Word 2007, and PowerPoint 2007 documents, and **Office Styles** ensure a consistent appearance among the diagrams, tables, and shapes.

To transfer information between Office programs, or many other Windows programs for that matter, you copy, move, link, embed, or hyperlink information depending on the imposed situation, as follows:

Imposed Situation	Method to Adopt
Inserted information will not need updating.	Copy or move
Inserted information needs to be automatically updated in the destination file as changes are made to the data in the source file, or Source file will always be available and you want to minimise the size of your file.	Link
Source file not always accessible, or Destination file needs to be edited without the changes showing in the source file.	Embed
To jump to a location in a document or Web page, or to a file in a different program.	Hyperlink

The improved charting capabilities in Excel are shared across the main Office programs, so you can create and interact with charts the same way, whichever program you are using. You can build tables, charts, and create **SmartArt** in Excel with the same tools you use in Word and PowerPoint.

Copying or Moving Information

To copy or move information between Office 2007 programs is extremely easy. Most of the time you can just drag and drop a selection between programs. It is safer to do this with the right mouse button depressed, as you are usually given the option to **Move** or **Copy**. This prevents you actually deleting something from the source document, when you only wanted to copy it.

To illustrate the technique, we will copy the file **Project 3**, created in Excel, into a Word document. Let's first assume that we only have the source file **Project 3** on disc, and don't have Excel on the computer. In such a situation, you can only copy the whole file into Word. To achieve this, do the following:

- Start Word and minimise it on the Taskbar.

- Click the **Computer** option on the **Start** menu and locate the file whose contents you want to copy into Word.

- Click the filename that you want to copy, hold the mouse button down and point to Word on the Taskbar until the application opens.

- While still holding the mouse button down, move the mouse pointer into Word's open document to where you want to insert the contents of **Project 3**.

- Release the mouse button to place the contents of the Excel file into Word at that point.

The result of this operation is shown in Fig. 9.1 below.

Fig. 9.1 A Copied Spreadsheet in Word 2007.

Source File and Application Available

If you have Office 2007 installed you should have both Excel and Word on your PC, so you should have both the file and the application that created it on your computer. You can then copy all or part of the contents of the source file to the destination file, as follows:

- Start Excel and open **Project 3.xlsx**, select the information to copy and click the **Home**, **Clipboard**, **Copy** button.

- Start Word, locate where you want the insertion and click the **Home**, **Clipboard**, **Paste** button. Then select the first **Keep Source Formatting** option from the menu that opens when you click the Paste Options Smart Tag, as shown in Fig. 9.2 on the next page.

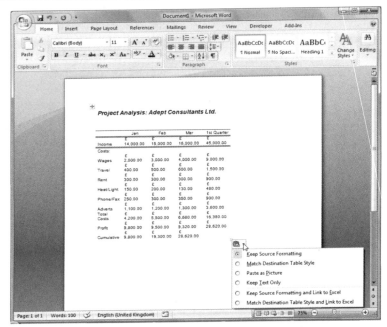

Fig. 9.2 Completing a Paste into Word 2007.

The worksheet is pasted as a table in Word and you will need to increase the width of its columns to force the £ signs to display on the same line as the numeric values.

Object Linking and Embedding

Object Linking is copying information from one file (the source file) to another file (the destination file) and maintaining a connection between the two files. When information in the source file is changed, then the information in the destination file is automatically updated. Linked data is stored in the source file, while the file into which you place the data stores only the location of the source and displays a representation of the linked data.

For example, you would use Object Linking if you wanted an Excel chart included in a Word document to be updated whenever the data in Excel was changed. The Excel worksheet containing the chart would be referred to as the source file, while the Word document would be referred to as the destination file.

Object Embedding is inserting information created in one file (the source file) into another file (the container file). After it is embedded, the object becomes part of the container file. When you double-click an embedded object, it opens in the application in which it was created in the first place. You can then edit it in place, and the original object in the source application remains unchanged.

Thus, the main differences between linking and embedding are where the data is stored and how it is updated after you place it in your file. Linking saves you disc space as only one copy of the linked object is kept on disc. Embedding a logo in the Word template used for your headed paper, would save the logo every time a letter was saved, whereas linking it would not.

Linking Selected Information

To link selected information from an existing file created in one application into another, do the following:

- Select the information in the source file you want to link and click the **Home**, **Clipboard**, **Copy** button, or **Ctrl+C**.

- In the destination file, locate where you want the insertion placed and click the **Home**, **Clipboard**, **Paste** button. Then select the first **Keep Source Formatting and Link to ...** option from the menu that opens when you click the Paste Options Smart Tag, as shown earlier in Fig. 9.2.

Embedding Selected Information

To embed selected information from an existing file created in one application into another, do the following:

- Select the information in the source file you want to link and click the **Copy** button, or **Ctrl+C**.

- In the destination file, locate where you want the insertion placed and click the **Paste Special** button. Select the type of object involved in the **As** list as shown in Fig. 9.3, where we were embedding a selection from an Excel worksheet.

Fig. 9.3 Using Paste Special to Embed an Object.

- To embed the object, make sure the **Paste** option button is selected and click **OK**.

- The **Paste link** option button gives you another way of linking the object.

- The **Display as icon** check box, places an icon, which you can double-click to open the object data in the source file application.

An Excel Chart in PowerPoint

As an example, we will link an Excel chart into a PowerPoint presentation, to be shown, say, in a slide show. Furthermore, if the chart data changes, the chart in PowerPoint will be updated automatically. To do this, select the chart in Excel and click the **Home**, **Clipboard**, **Copy** button, or **Ctrl+C**. Open PowerPoint 2007, create an empty slide (**New Slide**, **Blank** command) and click the **Paste** button, or **Ctrl+V**, to paste the chart onto it.

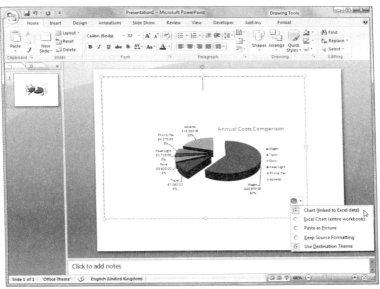

Fig. 9.4 Linking an Excel Chart to a PowerPoint Slide.

In the lower-right corner the **Paste Options** button should appear. Click this and confirm that the **Chart (linked to Excel data)** menu option is selected, as shown in Fig. 9.4 above. This links the chart and ensures that any changes in Excel will be reflected in PowerPoint.

Hypertext Links

All the Office 2007 applications support hyperlinks. A hyperlink causes a jump to another location in the current document or Web page, to a different document or Web page, or to a file that was created in a different program. For example, you can jump from an Excel worksheet to a Word document or to a PowerPoint slide, to see more detail.

A hyperlink is represented by a 'hot' image or by display text (which is often blue and underlined) that you click to jump to a different location. To insert a hyperlink into Excel, Word, or PowerPoint, select the display text or image in the application, and click the **Insert**, **Links**, **Insert Hyperlink** button 🔗 Hyperlink to open the dialogue box shown below, in which you can browse for the destination file, or enter a Web site URL address.

To illustrate the procedure, start Excel, open the **Project 4** file, and type in cell B16 the words 'Yearly Costs', as shown in Fig. 9.5 below.

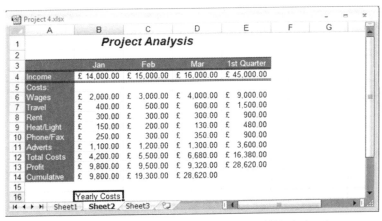

Fig. 9.5 Creating a Hyperlink in an Excel Worksheet.

While cell B16 is the active cell, click the **Insert**, **Links**, **Hyperlink** button and locate the **Project 9** file in the displayed Insert Hyperlink dialogue box shown in Fig. 9.6 below. Once you have located the file, its name is inserted in the **Address** box, and pressing the **OK** button inserts a hyperlink to that location.

Fig. 9.6 Locating the Address for a Hyperlink.

Fig. 9.7 The Select Place in Document Dialogue Box.

Should you want to jump to a specific sheet or defined name within a workbook, click the **Bookmark** button which opens the Select Place in Document dialogue box shown in Fig. 9.7. In the latter case, when you jump to the specified document, the cell range of the selected defined name will be highlighted automatically, a rather useful feature.

Pressing the **OK** button of each dialogue box, underlines the text in B16, as shown in Fig 9.8 on the next page, and changes its colour to blue.

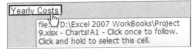

Fig. 9.8 The Hyperlink Address.

Pointing to such a hyperlink changes the mouse pointer to a hand, as shown here in Fig. 9.8. Left-clicking it opens the 'Charts' sheet of the **Project 9** file. When you have finished looking at this file, click the **Close** icon on the worksheet, shown in Fig. 9.9 below, for the program to return you automatically to the hyperlinked Excel workbook.

Fig. 9.9 The Close Button in the Excel Window.

If the location of the file you wanted to hyperlink to is incorrect, then errors will obviously occur.

To remove unwanted hyperlinks, right-click the hyperlinked cell, then select the **Remove Hyperlink** option from the displayed menu.

As you can see from the above discussion, hyperlinks can just as easily be created and used on Web pages, provided you have Internet access. The procedure is identical to creating a hyperlink between two files on your hard disc.

Hypertext links on a Web page are elements that you can click with the left mouse button to jump to another Web document. You are actually fetching another file to your PC, and the link is an address that uniquely identifies the location of the target file, wherever it may be. This address is known as a Uniform Resource Locator (URL for short).

How to use Excel on the Internet is the subject of the rest of this chapter.

Sharing with Others

Microsoft has integrated Excel 2007 with the Internet and the Web by allowing the creation of the following:

- Non-interactive data or charts.

- Interactive spreadsheets, PivotTable lists, and charts.

- Combination Web pages.

The first one of these lets users view data as they would in Microsoft Excel, including tabs for each worksheet that they can click to switch between worksheets. It is like publishing a 'snapshot' of the data, but users cannot interact with the data.

To view non-interactive data or charts on the Web, users only need a Web browser – there are no restrictions on the type of browser. Also, they don't need Excel 2007 on their computer.

The last two items on the list above allow the user to interact with all or some of the data on your Web page. Such a Web page is created from an Excel worksheet, or items from it, by saving the data with 'spreadsheet functionality'. Publishing in this way allows users to enter, format, calculate, analyse, sort and filter data.

Interactive Web pages allow users to change the data and layout of Web page items. They are used if you have data that users want to recalculate. For example, if you are supplying a program to calculate the repayments on loans based on particular interest rates (to be discussed shortly).

To view interactive (or partially interactive) data on the Web, users need to have installed on their computer one of the latest versions of the Microsoft Internet Explorer (preferably version 6 or later).

Creating Excel Static Web Pages

Most Web pages are written in HTML (Hypertext Markup Language), which can be used by Web browsers on any operating system, such as Windows, Macintosh, and UNIX.

Entire Workbook on a Web Page

Excel allows you to put an entire workbook on a Web page. As an example, we will use the **Project 9** file which has several worksheets, including three charts saved in a Chart sheet. To do this, start Excel, then

- Open **Project 9**, and use the **Office** button and select the **Save As** option. In the **Save as type** box of the displayed dialogue box select **Web Page** which changes the displayed dialogue box.

- In the **Address Bar** at the top of the window, locate the drive, folder, Web folder, Web server, or File Transfer Protocol (FTP) location where you want to save your Web page (we chose our WorkBooks folder).

- Make sure that the **Entire Workbook** radio button is selected, then click the **Change Title** button to display the Set Page Title dialogue box, as shown in Fig. 9.10 on the next page. Type a description which will be displayed in the Title bar of the browser.

- Finally, press the **Save** button. To see the result of your efforts, then locate the **.htm** file produced by the save command. In our case this file was called **Project 9.htm** by default.

- Locating and double-clicking this file opens it in your browser, as shown in Fig. 9.11, also on the next page.

Fig. 9.10 Saving a Workbook as a Web Page.

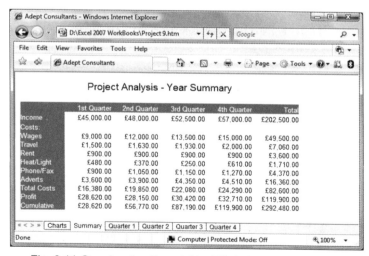

Fig. 9.11 Opening the Saved .htm File in Internet Explorer.

Note the workbook tabs at the bottom of your browser window. These are similar to the tabs of an Excel workbook, except that when you point at them with the mouse pointer their full path is displayed in the Status bar.

Most of the features and formatting in your workbook are retained when you open your Web page (**.htm**) file later. These are held in a **_files** folder, called the 'supporting files folder' (in our case **Project 9_files)**. If you ever move the Web page (**.htm**) from the place it was saved in the first place, you must also move the supporting files (**_files**) folder, otherwise you will lose all features and formatting when viewing your work on your browser.

Also, if you want to change data in your Web site, update the original **.xlsx** file in Excel and then republish it. We will discuss how to do this automatically shortly.

Single Worksheet on a Web Page

Excel allows you to put a single worksheet on a Web page. As an example, we will use the **Project 8** file, then use the **Office** button and select the **Save As** option. In the **Save as type** box of the displayed dialogue box select **Single File Web Page** which changes the displayed dialogue box, then

- Make sure that the **Selection: Sheet** radio button is chosen which causes the default **Items on Summary** name to appear in the **Choose** box. Next, click the **Change Title** button to display the Set Page Title dialogue box and type a description which will be displayed in the Title bar of the window, as shown in Fig. 9.12 on the next page.

- Next, click the **Open published web page in browser** check box and press the **Publish** button.

Fig. 9.12 Saving a Single Worksheet as a Web Page.

- Excel formats your chosen worksheet into a Web page and displays it in your browser, as shown in Fig. 9.13.

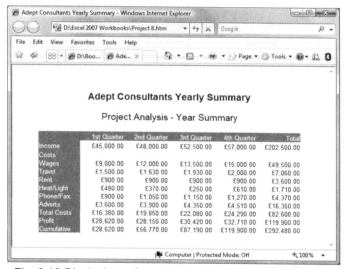

Fig. 9.13 Displaying a Saved Web Page in Internet Explorer.

Auto-Republishing Web Pages

To illustrate this procedure, first construct an Excel example suitable for Web page auto-republishing. We chose below to create a loans repayment worksheet using the compound interest formula given as

$$A = P * (1+R/100)^Y$$

where P is the principal (original money) lent, and A is what it amounts to in time Y years at an interest rate R% per annum.

We carry out the calculation on a yearly basis to the full period of the loan of 15 years which cannot be varied, with a value of Principal of £30,000 and with an interest rate of 5%, both of which can be varied by the user in cells C4 and C3 respectively. Cells A9:A23 hold the period of the loan, while cells C9:C23 hold the result of the calculation. Hint – type in C9 the Excel formula =$C$4*(1+$C$3/100)^A9, then copy it into C10:C23.

The resultant Excel worksheet, including a line chart of the repayment amount at the end of each year, is shown in Fig. 9.14 below.

Fig. 9.14 Creating an Interactive Excel Web Page.

Next, use the **Office** button and select the **Save As** option. In the **Save as type** box of the displayed dialogue box select **Web Page** which changes the displayed dialogue box, as shown in Fig. 9.15.

Fig. 9.15 Saving an Interactive Web Page.

Then follow the procedure discussed previously, namely, in the **Address Bar** at the top of the window, give the location where you want to save your Web page (we chose our WorkBooks folder), then make sure that the **Selection: Sheet** radio button is selected, and press the **Publish** button.

Finally, in the displayed Publish as Web Page dialogue box, shown in Fig. 9.16 on the next page, check both the **AutoRepublish every time this workbook is saved** box and the **Open published web page in browser** box, and press the **Publish** button.

Fig. 9.16 The Publish as Web Page Dialogue Box.

What displays next, is shown in Fig. 9.17 below.

Fig. 9.17 A Published Excel Sheet in Internet Explorer.

Users cannot change the worksheet directly on their Web browser, but when changes are made in Excel by the originator to the worksheet, these changes appear on the Web page and the chart is updated automatically.

10

Excel Macro Basics

A macro is simply a set of instructions made up of a sequence of keystrokes, mouse selections, or commands stored in a macro file. After saving, or writing, a macro and attaching a quick key combination to it, you can run the same sequence of commands whenever you want. This can save a lot of time and, especially with repetitive operations, can save mistakes creeping into your work.

In Excel there are two basic ways of creating macros. The first one involves using Microsoft Visual Basic, the programming language that is common to all Office applications. With this method, you can write quite complex macro programs directly into a macro file using the Visual Basic editor which allows you, amongst other facilities, to edit, copy, or rename macros. Understanding Visual Basic also makes it easier to program with other Microsoft applications that use the language.

For simple work however, you don't really have to learn to program in Visual Basic, as Excel includes a Macro Recorder which provides you with the second method of generating macros. The Macro Recorder stores the actions you take, including mouse clicks, and the commands you use while working with Excel, which can then be played back (run) to repeat the recorded actions and commands.

Before you record or write a macro, plan the steps and commands you want the macro to perform. This is essential, because if you make a mistake while recording the macro, corrections you make will also be recorded.

Using the Macro Recorder

We will now use the worksheet saved under **Project 3** (see page 62) to show how we can use Excel's Macro Recorder to create a macro to perform 'what-if' type of projections by, say, increasing the 'Wages' bill by 15%.

If you haven't saved **Project 3** on disc, it will be necessary for you to enter the information shown in Fig. 10.1 into Excel so that you can benefit from what is to be introduced at this point. If you have saved **Project 3**, click the **Office** button, select the **Open** option from the displayed menu, locate the file and double-click it to open it. Your display should look similar to the one below.

Fig. 10.1 An Example to Demonstrate Using the Macro Recorder.

What we would like to do now is to edit the entry in cell B6 under 'Wages' so that it can be increased by 15%. One way of doing this would be to multiply the contents of the cell value by 1.15. But please don't do anything to your worksheet yet, just read.

To change the value in cell B6 by 15%, we would start by changing its contents into a formula, by pressing the **F2** function key to 'Edit' the value in it by adding an equals sign at the beginning of the entry and then typing ***1.15** at the end of it, which has the effect of multiplying the contents of the cell by 1.15, thus increasing its contents by 15%. We would then press the **Enter** key which would cause the cell pointer to drop to B7, press the ⇧ arrow key to move back to cell B6, then press the ⇨ arrow key to move to cell C6.

The exact steps you will have to take in creating this macro, after highlighting cell B6, are as follows:

Press **F2** to 'Edit' cell
Press the **Home** key to move to beginning of entry
Type **=** to change entry to formula
Press **End** to move to the end of the entry
Type ***1.15**
Press the **Enter** key
Press ⇧arrow key
Press ⇨ arrow key.

However, before starting to record a macro, and before you open the file in which this macro is to be created, we need to change the macro security in Excel. To do this, start Excel then click the **Developer**, **Code**, **Macro Security** button to open the Trust Center screen (if the **Developer** tab is not shown on the Ribbon, please refer to page 139 on how to install the add-in). Then, under **Macro Settings**, select the **Enable all macros** radio button, and under **Developer Macro Settings** check the **Trust access to the VBA project object model**.

Recording an Excel Macro

Having opened the **Project 3** file, select cell B6 - the first cell we want to operate on. Then, click the **View**, **Macros**, **Macros** button, and select the **Record Macro** option from the drop-down menu. This opens the Record Macro dialogue box with the default **Macro name** given as Macro1.

The macro name in the Record Macro dialogue box can be changed by you to some more meaningful name, if you so wish. We then specify that the **Shortcut key** in the Record Macro dialogue box should be **Ctrl+w** (**w** for wages), as shown in Fig. 10.2 below.

Fig. 10.2 Starting the Recording of a Macro.

You can also type an appropriate message in the
Description box so you know what the macro does. In
this case we typed 'Increasing cell B6 by 15%', because
our macro is designed to only change the first wages cell.

Pressing the **OK** button, starts Macro Recording, and
puts a **Macros**
button on the
Status   Bar
shown here.

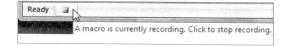

Everything you type from now on becomes part of the
macro. To start recording our macro, press/type the
appropriate key/information, as shown below.

F2
Home
=
End
*1.15
Enter
Press ⇧arrow key
Press ⇨arrow key

To stop recording the macro, click the **Macro** button on
the **Status Bar**, or click the **View**, **Macros**, **Macros**, **Stop
Recording** Ribbon command.

To see the Visual Basic code of your macro, click the
View, **Macros**, **Macros** button and select the **View
Macros** option from the drop-down menu (or use the
Alt+F8 shortcut), specify which macro you want to edit by
highlighting it, and press the **Edit** button on the Macro
dialogue box to display the code shown in Fig. 10.3 on
the next page.

However, before executing this macro, activate
worksheet **Project 3.xlsx** and change the entry in cell B6
back to its original value of 2000 (it was changed by 15%
while you were typing the latest macro commands).

Fig. 10.3 The Visual Basic Code of our Macro.

Next, save this macro with the worksheet, but select the **Excel Macro-Enabled Workbook** extension **.xlsm** in the **Save as type** box. We also saved this workbook under the new filename **Autopro 1**, because had we used the same filename it would be rather difficult to distinguish between the two file extensions **(.xlsm** and **.xlsx)**.

Should things go wrong when you execute your macro, reopen the original **Project 3.xlsx** worksheet and start again rather than attempting to correct the **Autopro 1.xlsm** file.

To run the first macro, place the cell pointer on cell B6, then press **Ctrl+w**. The shortcut key starts the macro and automatically changes the entry in B6 by 15% from 2000 to 2300.

Visual Basic Programming Advantages

When the macros you write become more complicated there are many advantages to using Visual Basic rather than using the macro command language that much earlier versions of Excel and other spreadsheet packages used.

In Visual Basic you can assign values directly to variables instead of storing a value in a name as you would have to do in the macro command language. Variables can be made available to all procedures, to just the procedure in a module, or to just a single procedure, thus being far more flexible than names. In addition, in Visual Basic you can define constants to hold static values that you refer to repeatedly.

Reading Visual Basic Code

Referring to our simple example, you can see that Visual Basic has created a macro that is preceded by comment statements (that start with an apostrophe (')) in which you are informed of the name of the macro, the comment you typed in, and the keyboard shortcut.

The macro commands are placed in between the two keywords **Sub** and **End Sub** which mark the beginning and end of a macro. In general, keywords, variables, operators, and procedure calls are referred to as statements which are instructions to perform an action.

The statement

ActiveCell.FormulaR1C1 = "=2000*1.15"

is the way that Visual Basic enters the formula **=2000*1.15** into the active cell. In Visual Basic terminology; it uses the **Range** object to identify the range you want to change and sets the **Formula** property of the range to assign a formula to the range.

An 'object' is something you control in Visual Basic. Each object has characteristics called 'properties' which control the appearance of the object. Objects also have 'methods' which are actions that they can take. In Visual Basic you use:

- Objects (such as Workbooks, Worksheets, Ranges, Charts) to perform a task. Each object has characteristics, called properties, that make that object useful by controlling the appearance or behaviour of an object.

- Properties (such as ActiveCell, ActiveSheet, Value, Selection, ColumnWidth, RowHeight) to examine the condition of an object by returning the value of one of the object's properties (such as a numeric value for ColumnWidth, True, or False).

- Methods which are actions that objects can do (such as Calculate, Clear, Copy, Justify, or Table). Methods are a part of objects just like properties. The difference between them is that properties have values which are set or returned, while methods are actions you would like an object to perform.

Should you want to learn to program in Visual Basic, then may we suggest you start with the book *Using Visual Basic* (BP498), also published by BERNARD BABANI (publishing) Ltd.

Editing a Macro

A macro can be edited by opening the file that contains it and pressing **Alt+F8** to display the Macro dialogue box, then selecting the required macro and pressing the **Edit** button, as discussed earlier.

Since each of the three months in our worksheet is to be changed we can edit all Macro1 references by copying the highlighted entries and pasting them twice before the **End Sub** statement as shown in Fig. 10.4.

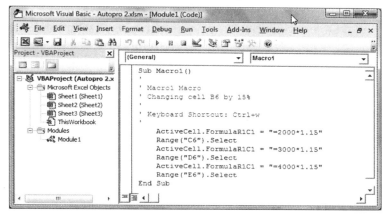

Fig. 10.4 Editing a Macro.

In Fig. 10.4 we have also changed references made to the amount of wages in the **ActiveCell.Formula** command, and typed the correct cell reference in **Range().Select** command. We then saved the workbook under the filename **Autopro 2**.

Doing so also saves the new **Macro1** within the **Autopro 2** file. If your macro is correct, activating cell B6 and pressing **Ctrl+w** runs it and increases by 15% the values of the wages entries for the three months from those shown on the original worksheet in Fig. 10.1 on page 170.

We could use the same macro to find out the effect of increasing wages by different percentages by editing it, but this would be rather inefficient. A better method is to allocate a cell for the % increase, say cell G5, and edit the macro so that reference to that cell is made in the R1C1 absolute format.

In our example, from cell B6 we would have to refer to R[-1]C[5] (Row 1 above present position, Column 5 from present position) which is the reference to cell G5 from B6.

Finally, edit all macro references and save the worksheet under the file name **Autopro 3**. Running the macro now changes the worksheet entries to those shown in Fig. 10.5 below.

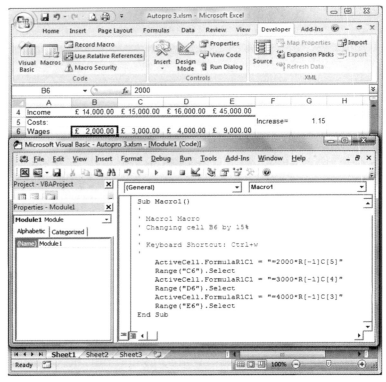

Fig. 10.5 A Macro Incorporating a Percentage Increase Cell.

Macro Interaction with Keyboard

A further addition to the above macros could be made to allow for user entry of the 'increment' value from the keyboard, rather than having to edit cell G5. This can be achieved by using the **InputBox()** macro command, which creates a dialogue box, as shown below, and returns the information entered into it.

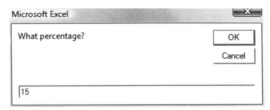

Fig. 10.6 The Input Box.

The general format of this macro command is:

Variable = InputBox("message")

and it returns the value typed on the keyboard into the *variable*.

In the macro shown on the next page we have tried to show the power of Visual Basic without making the example too complicated. First, you are asked to give a percentage rate, then the macro calculates the increment and places the value of rate in G5 and stores the original contents of B6:D6 into the three variables, Xjan, Xfeb, and Xmar.

Next, the calculations take place and the results are entered in cell range B6:D6. Finally, a dialogue box is displayed (it can be moved out of the way) asking you to press the **OK** button in order to restore the original contents to the 'Wages' cell range, and change the contents of G5 to 0 (zero).

Note: This macro only works if the active worksheet is **Sheet1** when you start the macro. If the active sheet is the macro module, then a run time error is encountered.

Finally, save this workbook as **Autopro 4** before attempting to run it.

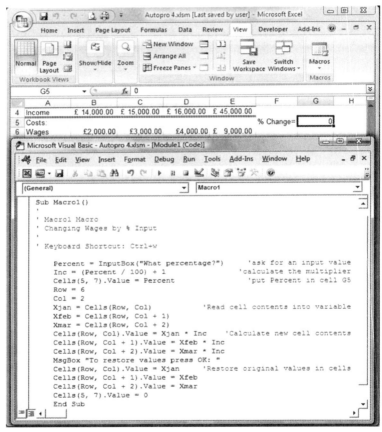

Fig. 10.7 A Macro Incorporating an Input Box.

To start the macro, activate cell B6 and press **Ctrl+w**.

Visual Basic has many more statements, commands and functions which can be used to build and run your application in special ways. What we have tried to do here is to introduce you to the subject and give you some idea of the power of this programming language.

* * *

That is about it. We hope you have enjoyed reading this book as much as we have enjoyed writing it. Of course Excel 2007 is capable of a lot more than we have discussed here, but what we have tried to do is to give you enough information so that you can forge ahead and explore by yourself the rest of its capabilities.

What follows next is a chapter of exercises with enough guidance to help you get going on your own, followed by a chapter that lists all the functions available to Excel 2007 with an explanation of their required parameters. Finally, we also include a glossary of terms for reference, and in case you have trouble with any jargon that may have crept in.

* * *

11

Exercises Using Excel

The following exercises will help you to get going on your own and might be of interest to you. We give you as much guidance as we think is needed for you to complete them by yourself. Good luck!

Compound Interest

To illustrate the behaviour of interest rates, set up an Excel worksheet as shown in Fig. 11.1 below, to calculate the compound interest of money lent over a certain period of time. Plot the resultant yearly interest against time, on the same graph, for three different values of interest rates.

Fig. 11.1 The Layout of the Compound Interest Example.

Compound interest is calculated using the formula

A = P * (1+R/100)^Y

where P is the principal (original money) lent, and A is what it amounts to in time Y years at an interest rate R% per annum. The cumulative interest charged is A-P.

Carry out the above calculation on a yearly basis to the full period of the loan (N=25) years, with a constant value of Principal (P=£30,000), but with variable values of interest rate R, namely 7.5, 10 and 12.5%.

Type in your formulae in the worksheet in such a way (by making absolute reference to cells E3 to E5) as to allow you to copy these in the rows below the 'number of years' range that stretches from column G to column AE. You should then only need to change the value of R for the required 'Yearly Interest' to be calculated automatically in row 10.

Use the **Home**, **Editing, Fill, Series** command to fill the 'Number of Years' range with incremental data, and the **Home**, **Clipboard, Copy** button and **Home**, **Clipboard**, **Paste**, **Paste Special, Values** button to copy the values of 'Yearly Interest' for each value of R to the bottom of the sheet for subsequent graphing. Copying by value is necessary to avoid changes to the data when R is changed.

Format your worksheet as shown in Fig. 11.1 on the previous page (or better), and use the information in cells A12:A14 plus F12:T14, by first highlighting the first cell block then pressing the **Ctrl** key down and, while keeping it depressed, highlighting the second cell block. Next, in the **Insert**, **Charts** group, select the chart of your choice and specify Sheet2 as the placement area.

Note that you might have to change the font size of the title, axes labels, and legends, and also re-size the chart to get what is shown in Fig. 11.2 on the next page.

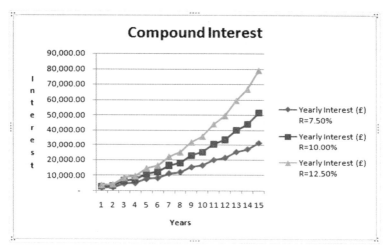

Fig. 11.2 A Graph of the Compound Interest Example.

Product Sales Calculations

The first column shown below holds the part numbers which identify a product, while the second and third columns hold the cost price and % profit required from the sale of each product. The fourth column holds information on the number of items sold, as follows:

Part No.	Cost Price (£)	% Profit	No. Sold
127	5.6	110	2500
130	6.5	130	1300
133	7	115	2800
136	6.25	125	1900
139	7.25	118	2300
142	7.5	135	2550
145	6.75	120	1800
148	6	133	3200

151	6.55	128	2750
154	7.55	122	1750
157	5.95	119	1950
160	6.16	124	2850

Assuming that the VAT rate is 17.5%, but can be changed subsequently to some other value, use Excel to calculate the following, assuming the relationships given below:

Sale price for each part,
VAT charged/unit,
Total income,
Sales cost,
Profit made.

Use the layout shown below for the input data, and the calculated results. You will need to enter the following relationships in columns I to M, respectively:

Column I:
Sale price_unit=Cost price_unit*(I+% profit_unit/100)*(I+VAT%/100)
Column J:
VAT charged_unit=Cost price_unit*(I+% profit_unit/100)*(VAT%/100)
Column K:
Total income=Sale price_unit * No. sold
Column L:
Total sales cost=(Cost price_unit+VAT charged_unit)*No. sold
Column M:
Profit made=(Sale price_unit*No. sold)–Sales cost.

Format your worksheet as shown below (or better), and make provision for displaying the 'Total Profit Made' and 'Total VAT Charged' to also be displayed in cells C8 and C9 respectively.

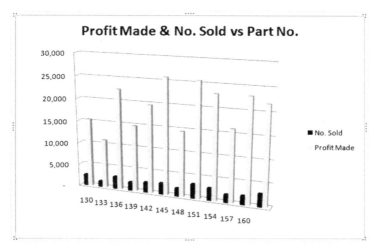

Fig. 11.3 The Layout of the Product Sales Calculations Example.

Having done so, define a graph (see Fig. 11.4 below) to plot profit made for each product and the corresponding volume of sales of each product versus the part number of the products. Annotate, title and save your graph on a separate worksheet of the workbook from that used for the calculations. See end of chapter for annotation method.

Fig. 11.4 A Graph of the Product Sales Calculations Example.

Salary Calculations

A firm employs several people who are identified by a unique works number, as shown in the sample table below. The first column of the table holds the works number which identifies a person, while the second column holds the gross annual salary (£) of that person. The third and fourth columns of the table hold information relating to the overtime worked (hrs) per month, and the corresponding hourly rate (£), respectively.

Employee Works No.	Annual Income	Overtime (hrs/month)	Overtime rate (£/hr)
7001	18850	14	14
7002	48500	10	29
7003	69750	6	40
7004	12900	18	16
7005	24350	6	17
7006	11900	12	12
7007	21000	16	15
7008	34850	8	21
7009	28350	11	19
7010	25480	9	18
7011	16750	15	13
7012	53100	4	32

In addition to the above, the company would also like to hold the following information for each employee;

Monthly Overtime Income,
Total Monthly N.I.,
Monthly Tax on Gross Yearly Income,
Monthly Tax on Overtime,
Total Monthly Income,
Total Monthly Tax.

We propose to use an Excel worksheet to calculate and hold this information. For simplicity we will assume that a person pays 11% of their monthly gross salary (excluding the first £5,000 and overtime) towards National Insurance (N.I.), while what is left after personal allowance and N.I. is taxed at 22%. In addition, all earnings on overtime are taxed at 40%.

Use the layout, labels and formatting suggested in Fig. 11.5 (or better) to carry out these calculations. Devise your own formulae for the required calculations.

Type in your formulae in the worksheet in such a way (by making absolute reference to cells C2 to C4) as to allow you to copy these easily. You should then only need to change the values of tax rates and/or N.I., for the information in the consolidated area of the worksheet (C9 to C11) to be calculated automatically.

Use the following input values:

Tax Rate X = 22%,
Tax Rate Y = 40%,
National Insurance = 11%,
Personal Allowance = £5,000.

Fig. 11.5 The Layout of the Salary Calculations Example.

Having achieved the above, define a stacked bar chart (see Fig. 11.6 below), to plot the Total Monthly Income, Total Monthly Tax, and Total Monthly N.I. versus Employee Works No. Annotate, title and save your chart within the workbook but on a different worksheet.

Fig. 11.6 A Graph of the Salary Calculations Example.

Procedure for Annotating a Chart

Fig. 11.7 The Select Data Source
Dialogue box.

To annotate a chart, select it, then click the **Design**, **Data**, **Select Data** button to display the Select Data Source dialogue box, then click the **Edit** button and select the range for the horizontal axis labels, and repeat this procedure to define the Legend labels.

12

Excel 2007 Functions

Excel's functions are built-in formulae that perform specialised calculations. Their general format is:

name(arg1,arg2,...)

where 'name' is the function name, and 'arg1', 'arg2', etc., are the arguments required for the evaluation of the function. Arguments must appear in a parenthesised list as shown above and their exact number depends on the function being used. However, some functions do not require arguments and are used without parentheses. Examples of these are: FALSE, NA, NOW, PI, RAND, TODAY and TRUE.

There are four types of arguments used with functions: numeric values, range values, string values and conditions, the type used being dependent on the type of function. Numeric value arguments can be entered either directly as numbers, as a cell address, a cell range name or as a formula. Range value arguments can be entered either as a range address or a range name, while string value arguments can be entered as an actual value (a string in double quotes), as a cell address, a cell name, or a formula. Condition arguments normally use logical operators or refer to an address containing a logic formula.

Types of Functions

There are several types of functions in Excel 2007, namely, financial, date and time, mathematical and trigonometric, statistical, lookup and reference, database, text, logical, and information. Each type of function requires its own number and type of arguments.

Function arguments, also known as parameters, are listed on the next few pages under the various function categories. To find out in detail how these functions can be used, click the **Formulas**, **Function Library**, **Insert Function** button (🔣) to display:

Fig. 12.1 The Insert Function Box.

You can either type a brief description of what you want to do in the search box or you can click the down arrow to the right of the select a category box to reveal all the available functions in Excel. Selecting a function from the drop-down list and clicking the **Help on this function** link at the bottom-left of the box, provides detailed help on the chosen function.

In Fig. 12.2 below the various function categories appear as books which when clicked display a drop-down menu of the actual functions in each category. The only function category that does not appear anywhere on this screen is the Database. We are sure this is an oversight!

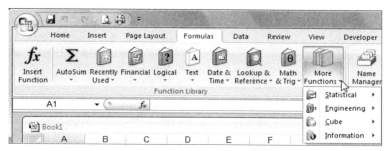

Fig. 12.2 The Function Library.

In what follows, we list all the functions and what they return in a concise form for ease of selection, and so that you can see at a glance what is available.

Cube Functions

Function	*Returns*
CUBEKPIMEMBER	A key performance indicator (KPI) property and displays the KPI name in the cell. A KPI is a quantifiable measurement, such as monthly gross profit or quarterly employee turnover, that is used to monitor an organisation's performance.
CUBEMEMBER	A member or tuple from the cube. Use to validate that the member or tuple exists in the cube.

CUBEMEMBERPROPERTY

> The value of a member property from the cube. Use to validate that a member name exists within the cube and to return the specified property for this member.

CUBERANKEDMEMBER

> The nth, or ranked, member in a set. Use to return one or more elements in a set, such as the top sales performer or the top 10 students.

CUBESET

> A calculated set of members or tuples by sending a set expression to the cube on the server, which creates the set, and then returns that set to Excel.

CUBESETCOUNT

> The number of items in a set.

CUBEVALUE

> An aggregated value from the cube.

Database Functions

Database functions perform calculations on a database. The database, called the input range, consists of records, which include fields and field names, like Fd below. A criterion range must be set up to select the records from the database that each function uses.

Function	Returns
DAVERAGE(Db,Fd,Cr)	The average of the values in the field Fd that meet the criteria Cr in a database Db.
DCOUNT(Db,Fd,Cr)	The number of non-blank cells in the field Fd that meet the criteria Cr in a database Db.

DCOUNTA(Db,Fd,Cr)	Counts non-blank cells from a specified database and criteria.
DGET(Db,Fd,Cr)	The single value in the field Fd that meets the criteria Cr in a database Db.
DMAX(Db,Fd,Cr)	The maximum value in the field Fd that meets the criteria Cr in a database Db.
DMIN(Db,Fd,Cr)	The minimum value in the field Fd that meets the criteria Cr in a database Db.
DPRODUCT(Db,Fd,Cr)	The result of the product of the values in the field Fd that meet the criteria Cr in a database Db.
DSTDEV(Db,Fd,Cr)	The standard deviation based on the values in the field Fd that meet the criteria Cr in a database Db.
DSTDEVP(Db,Fd,Cr)	The standard deviation based on the entire population of the values in the field Fd that meet the criteria Cr in a database Db.
DSUM(Db,Fd,Cr)	The sum of the values in the field Fd that meet the criteria Cr in a database Db.
DVAR(Db,Fd,Cr)	The estimated variance based on the values in the field Fd that meet the criteria Cr in a database Db.
DVARP(Db,Fd,Cr)	The variance based on the entire population of the values in the field Fd that meet the criteria Cr in a database Db.

Date and Time Functions

These generate and use serial numbers with dates having integer serial numbers between 1 and 65380 to represent dates between 1 January 1900 and 31 December 9999, and time having decimal serial numbers starting with 0.000 at midnight and ending with 0.99999 next midnight. The various functions are:

Function	*Returns*
DATE(Yr,Mh,Dy)	The date number of argument Yr,Mh,Dy.
DATEVALUE(Ts)	The number of days from 1 January 1900 of date string Ts.
DAY(Dn)	The day of the month number (1-31) of date number Dn.
DAYS360(Sn,En)	The number of days between Sn and En, based on a year of 12 months, each of 30 days.
EDATE(Sd,Ms)	The serial number of the date that is the indicated number of months Ms before or after the start date Sd.
EOMONTH(Sd,Ms)	The serial number of the last day of the month before or after a specified number of months Ms from the start date Sd.
HOUR(Tn)	The hour number (0-23) of time number Tn.
MINUTE(Tn)	The minute number (0-59) of time number Tn.
MONTH(Dn)	The month number (1-12) of date number Dn.

NETWORKDAYS(Sd,Ed)	The number of whole workdays between a start date Sd and an end date Ed.
NOW()	The serial number for the current date and time.
SECOND(Tn)	The second number (0-59) of time number Tn.
TIME(Hr,Ms,Ss)	The time number of argument Hr,Ms,Ss.
TIMEVALUE(Ts)	The time number of string Ts.
TODAY()	The current date number.
WEEKDAY(Dn)	The day of the week from date number Dn in integer form; 0 (Monday) through 6 (Sunday).
WEEKNUM(Sn)	The number that indicates where the week falls numerically within a year of a specified date Sn.
WORKDAY(Sd,Ds)	The number that represents a date that is the indicated number of working days Ds before or after a starting date Sd.
YEAR(Dn)	Returns the year number (0-199) of date number Dn.
YEARFRAC(Sd,Ed)	The year fraction representing the number of whole days between start date Sd and end date Ed.

External Functions

External functions are loaded with add-in programs.

Function	*Returns*
EUROCONVERT(Nr,Se,Tt)	The number of Euros in currency value Nr of an EU single currency member, the currency value of an EU single currency member of Nr Euros, or the currency value of an EU single currency member from the currency value Nr of another EU single currency member by using the Euro as an intermediary. Se is a three-letter string that represents the source currency code (DEM for Germany, FRF for France, EUR for Euro, etc.), while Tt is a similar three-letter target currency code, or cell reference, to which you want to convert.
SQL.REQUEST(Ed,Qt)	An array of query results or the number of rows affected by the query Qt of an external data source Ed (a string specifying data source name, user ID, and password).

Engineering Functions

Engineering functions mainly convert a number from one measurement system to another.

Function	*Returns*
BESSELI(x,n)	The modified Bessel function In(x) of order n evaluated at point x.

BESSELJ(x,n)	The Bessel function Jn(x) of order n evaluated at point x.
BESSELK(x,n)	The modified Bessel function Kn(x) of order n evaluated at point x.
BESSELY(x,n)	The Bessel function Yn(x) of order n evaluated at point x.
BIN2DEC(Nr)	The decimal number of a binary number Nr.
BIN2HEX(Nr)	The hexadecimal of a binary number Nr.
BIN2OCT(Nr)	The octal of a binary number Nr.
COMPLEX(Rn,In)	A complex number of real Rn and imaginary In coefficients.
CONVERT(Nr,Ut1,Ut2)	The conversion of a number Nr of units Ut1 of one measurement system to units Ut2 of another.
DEC2BIN(Nr)	The binary of a decimal number Nr.
DEX2HEX(Nr)	The hexadecimal of a decimal number Nr.
DEC2OCT(Nr)	The octal of a decimal number Nr.
DELTA(Nt1,Nt2)	Tests whether two values Nt1 and Nt2 are equal.
ERF(Ll,Ul)	The error function integrated between lower limit Ll and upper limit Ul.
ERFC(x)	The complementary error function integrated between x and infinity.

GESTEP(Nr,Sp)	Tests whether a number Nr is greater than a threshold value step value Sp.
HEX2BIN(Nr)	The binary of a hexadecimal number Nr.
HEX2DEC(Nr)	The decimal of a hexadecimal number Nr.
HEX2OCT(Nr)	The octal of a hexadecimal number Nr.
IMABS(Cn)	The absolute value (modulus) of a complex number Cn.
IMAGINARY(Cn)	The imaginary coefficient of a complex number Cn.
IMARGUMENT(Cn)	The argument theta, an angle expressed in radians of a complex number Cn.
IMCONJUGATE(Cn)	The complex conjugate of a complex number Cn.
IMCOS(Cn)	The cosine of a complex number Cn.
IMDIV(Cn1,Cn2)	The quotient of two complex numbers Cn1 and Cn2.
IMEXP(Cn)	The exponential of a complex number Cn.
IMLN(Cn)	The natural logarithm of a complex number Cn.
IMLOG10(Cn)	The base-10 logarithm of a complex number Cn.
IMLOG2(Cn)	The base-2 logarithm of a complex number Cn.
IMPOWER(Cn, Nr)	A complex number Cn raised to an integer power Nr.
IMPRODUCT(Cn1,Cn2)	The product of two complex numbers Cn1 and Cn2.

IMREAL(Cn)	The real coefficient of a complex number Cn.
IMSIN(Cn)	The sine of a complex number.
IMSQRT(Cn)	The square root of a complex number Cn in x+iy text format.
IMSUB(Cn1,Cn2)	The difference between two complex numbers Cn1 and Cn2 in x+iy text format.
IMSUM(Cn1,Cn2,...)	The sum of complex numbers in x+iy text format.
OCT2BIN(Nr)	The binary of an octal number.
OCT2DEC(Nr)	The decimal of an octal number Nr.
OCT2HEX(Nr)	The hexadecimal of an octal number Nr.

Financial Functions

Financial functions evaluate loans, annuities, depreciation and cash flows over a period of time, using numeric arguments. Where an optional parameter [Tp] is given the function will calculate for either an ordinary annuity or an annuity due, depending on the value you specified for type Tp. Percentages should be entered either as a decimal (for example, 0.155) or with a percent sign (for example, 15.5%).

Function	*Returns*
ACCRINT(Id,Sd,Ed,Rt,Nr)	The accrued interest for a security that pays periodic interest, where Id is the security's issue date, Sd is the starting date, Ed the ending (settlement) date, Rt the annual coupon rate, and Nr the number of coupon payments per year.

ACCRINTM(Id,Md,Rt)   The accrued interest for a security that pays interest at maturity, where Id is the issue date, Md the maturity date, and Rt the annual coupon rate.

AMORDEGRC(Ct,Pd,Fp,Sg,Pd,Rt,Yb)
The depreciation for each accounting period by using a depreciation coefficient, where Ct is the cost of the asset, Pd the purchase date, Fp the date of the end of the first period, Sg the salvage value, Pd the period, Rt the rate of depreciation, and Yb the year basis to be used.

AMORLINC (Ct,Pd,Fp,Sg,Pd,Rt,Yb)
The depreciation for each accounting period, where Ct is the cost of the asset, Pd the purchase date, Fp the date of the end of the first period, Sg the salvage value, Pd the period, Rt the rate of depreciation, and Yb the year basis to be used.

COUPDAYBS(Sd,Md,Nr)   The number of days from the beginning of the coupon period to the settlement date, where Sd is the settlement date, Md the maturity date, and Nr the number of coupon payments per year.

COUPDAYS(Sd,Md,Nr)   The number of days in the coupon period that contains the settlement date Sd, where Md is the maturity date, and Nr the number of coupon payments per year.

COUPDAYSNC(Sd,Md,Nr) The number of days from the settlement date to the next coupon date, where Sd is the settlement date, Md the maturity date, and Nr the number of coupon payments per year.

COUPNCD(Sd,Md,Nr) The next coupon date after the settlement date, where Sd is the settlement date, Md the maturity date, and Nr the number of coupon payments per year.

COUPNUM(Sd,Md,Nr) The number of coupons payable between the settlement date Sd and maturity date Md for Nr coupon payments per year.

COUPPCD(Sd,Md,Nr) The previous coupon date before the settlement date Sd of maturity date Md and Nr number of coupon payments per year.

CUMIPMT(Rt,Pp,Pv,Sd,Ed,Tp)
The cumulative interest paid on a loan of present value Pv between a starting date Sd and an ending date Ed at interest rate Rt, for a total number of payment periods of Pp. Tp is the timing of the payment (0 at end of period or 1 at beginning).

CUMPRINC(Rt,Pp,Pv,Sd,Ed,Tp)
The cumulative principal paid on a loan of present value Pv between a starting date Sd and an ending date Ed at interest rate Rt, for a total number of payment periods of Pp. Tp is the timing of the payment (0 at end of period or 1 at beginning).

DB(Ct,Sg,Lf,Pd)

The depreciation allowance of an asset with an initial value of Ct, life Lf, a final salvage value Sg for a specified period Pd, using the declining balance method.

DDB(Ct,Sg,Lf,Pd)

The double-declining depreciation allowance of an asset, with original cost Ct, predicted salvage value Sg, life Lf, and period Pd.

DISC(Sd,Md,Pr,Rv)

The discount rate for a security, where Sd is the settlement date, Md the maturity date, Pr the security's price per $100 face value, and Rv the redemption value per $100 face value.

DOLLARDE(Fd,Fn)

The dollar price expressed as a decimal number of a dollar price given as a fraction Fd with an Fn fraction denominator.

DOLLARFR(Dd,Fn)

The dollar price expressed as a fraction to a dollar price given as a decimal number with an Fn fraction denominator.

DURATION(Sd,Md,Cr,Ay,Nr)

The annual duration of a security with periodic interest payments, where Sd is the settlement date, Md the maturity date, Cr the security's annual coupon rate, Ay the annual yield, and Nr the number of coupon payments per year.

| EFFECT(Ni,Cy) | The effective annual interest rate given the annual nominal interest rate Ni, and the number of compounding periods per year Cy. |

| FV(Rt,Tm,Pt) | The future value of a series of equal payments, each of equal amount Pt, earning a periodic interest rate Rt, over a number of payment periods in term Tm. |

| FVSCHEDULE(Pr,Ir) | The future value of an initial principal Pr after applying a series of compound interest rates Ir. |

| INTRATE(Sd,Md,Ai,Ar) | The interest rate for a fully invested security, where Sd is the settlement date, Md the maturity date, Ai the amount invested, and Ar the amount to be received at maturity. |

| IPMT(Rt,Pr,Tm,Pv) | The interest payment for a given period Pr (between 1 and Tm) of a total term Tm of a loan with present value Pv at a constant interest rate Rt. |

| IRR(Rg,Gs) | The internal rate of return of range Rg of cash flows, based on the approximate percentage guess Gs. |

| ISPMT(Rt,Pr,Tm,Pv) | The interest paid during a specific period Pr (which must be between 1 and Tm) of a total term Tm of a loan with present value Pv at an interest rate Rt. |

MDURATION(Sd,Md,Cr,Ay,Nr)

The Macauley modified duration for a security with an assumed par value of $100, where Sd is the settlement date, Md the maturity date, Cr the security's annual coupon rate, Ay the annual yield, and Nr the number of coupon payments per year.

MIRR(Rg,Fr,Rr)

The modified internal rate of return for a series of cashflows in a range Rg, with interest rates Fr, paid on money used in cash flows and Rr received on reinvested cash flows.

NOMINAL(Er,Np)

The annual nominal interest rate, where Er is the effective interest rate, and Np the number of compounding periods per year.

NPER(Rt,Pt,Pv,Fv)

The number of periods required for a series of equal payments Pt, with a present value Pv, to accumulate a future value Fv, at a periodic interest rate Rt.

NPV(Rt,Rg)

The net present value of the series of future cash flows in range Rg, discounted at a periodic interest rate Rt.

ODDFPRICE(Sd,Md,Id,Fd,Rt,Ay,Rv,Nr)

The price per $100 face value of a security with an odd first period, where Sd is the settlement date, Md the maturity date, Id the security's issue date, Fd the first coupon date, Rt the interest rate, Ay the annual yield, and Nr the number of coupon payments per year.

ODDFYIELD(Sd,Md,Id,Fd,Rt,Sp,Rv,Nr)

The yield of a security with an odd first period, where Sd is the settlement date, Md the maturity date, Id the security's issue date, Fd the first coupon date, Rt the interest rate, Sp the security's price, Rv the redemption value per $100 face value, and Nr the number of coupon payments per year.

ODDLPRICE(Sd,Md,Id,Fd,Rt,Ay,Rv,Nr)

The price per $100 face value of a security with an odd last period, where Sd is the settlement date, Md the maturity date, Id the security's issue date, Fd the first coupon date, Rt the interest rate, Ay the annual yield, Rv the redemption value per $100 of face value, and Nr the number of coupon payments per year.

ODDLYIELD (Sd,Md,Id,Fd,Rt,Sp,Rv,Nr)

The yield of a security with an odd last period, where Sd is the settlement date, Md the maturity date, Id the security's issue date, Fd the first coupon date, Rt the interest rate, Sp the security price, Rv the redemption value per $100 of face value, and Nr the number of coupon payments per year.

PMT(Rt,Tm,Pv,Fv)

The payment on a loan with present value Pv, at interest rate Rt, for Tm number of payments and future value Fv.

PPMT(Rt,Pr,Tm,Pv,Fv)

The principal portion of the periodic payment on a loan of present value Pv, at interest rate Rt, for a number of payment periods Pr, leading to a future value Fv.

PRICE(Sd,Md,Rt,Ay,Rv,Nr)

The price per $100 face value of a security that pays periodic interest, where Sd is the settlement date, Md the maturity date, Rt the interest rate, Ay the security's annual yield, Rv the redemption value per $100 face value, and Nr the number of coupon payments per year.

PRICEDISC(Sd,Md,Dr,Rv)

The price per $100 face value of a discounted security, where Sd is the security's settlement date, Md the maturity date, Dr the discount rate, and Rv the redemption value.

PRICEMAT(Sd,Md,Id,Rt,Ay)

The price per $100 face value of a security that pays interest at maturity, where Sd is the security's settlement date, Md the maturity date, Id the issue date, Rt the interest rate, and Ay the security's annual yield.

PV(Rt,Tm,Pt)

The present value of a series of payments, each of amount Pt, discounted at a periodic interest rate Rt, over a number of payment periods in term Tm.

RATE(Tm,Pt,Pv,Fv)	The periodic interest rate necessary for a present value Pv to grow to a future value Fv, over the number of compounding periods in term Tm at Pt payments per period.
RECEIVED(Sd,Md,Ai,Dr)	The amount received at maturity for a fully invested security, where Sd is the Settlement date, Md the maturity date, Ai the amount invested, and Dr the security's discount rate.
SLN(Ct,Sg,Lf)	The straight line depreciation of an asset of cost Ct for one period, given its predicted salvage value Sg, and life Lf.
SYD(Ct,Sg,Lf,Pd)	The sum-of-years' digits depreciation of an asset of cost Ct, given its predicted salvage value Sg, life Lf, and period Pd.
TBILLEQ(Sd,Md,Dr)	The bond-equivalent yield for a Treasury bill, where Sd is the settlement date, Md the maturity date, and Dr the Treasury bill's discount rate.
TBILLPRICE(Sd,Md,Dr)	The price per $100 face value for a Treasury bill, where Sd is the settlement date, Md the maturity date, and Dr the Treasury bill's discount rate.
TBILLYIELD(Sd,Md,Pr)	The yield for a Treasury bill, where Sd is the settlement date, Md the maturity date, and Pr the Treasury bill's price per $100 face value.

VDB(Ct,Sg,Lf,S,E,*d*,*s*)

The depreciation of an asset of cost Ct, salvage value Sg, life Lf, over a period from start S to end E. Depreciation-factor *d* and switch *s*, are optional. If *s* is 1 it returns declining balance depreciation for life, else straight line is used after E.

XIRR(Cf,Pd)

The internal rate of return for a schedule of cash flows Cf that is not necessarily periodic, where Pd is a schedule of payment dates corresponding to the cash flow payments.

XNPV(Dr,Cf,Pd)

The net present value for a schedule of cash flows Cf that is not necessarily periodic, where Dr is the discount rate, and Pd the payment dates.

YIELD(Sd,Md,Rt,Pr,Rv,Nr)

The yield on a security that pays periodic interest , where Sd is the settlement date, Md the maturity date, Rt the interest rate, Pr the security's price per $100 face value, Rv the redemption value per $100 face value, and Nr the number of payments per year.

YIELDDISC(Sd,Md,Pr,Rv)

The annual yield for a discounted security; for example, a Treasury bill, where Sd is the settlement date, Md the maturity date, Pr the security's price per $100 face value, and Rv the redemption value per $100 face value.

YIELDMAT(Sd,Md,Id,Rt,Pr)

The annual yield of a security that pays interest at maturity, where Sd is the settlement date, Md the maturity date, Id the issue date, Rt the interest rate, and Pr the security's price per $100 face value.

Information Functions

Information functions perform a variety of advanced tasks, such as looking up values in a table, returning information about cells, ranges or the Excel environment.

Function	*Returns*
CELL(At,Rg)	The code representing the attribute At of range Rg.
ERROR.TYPE(X)	The error value.
INFO(At)	System information based on the attribute At.
ISBLANK(X)	The value 1 (TRUE), if X is an empty cell.
ISERR(X)	1 (TRUE), if X is an error value except #N/A.
ISERROR(X)	1 (TRUE), if X is any error.
ISEVEN(X)	1 (TRUE), if the number is even.
ISLOGICAL(X)	1 (TRUE), if X is a logical value.
ISNA(X)	1 (TRUE), if X contains #N/A.
ISNONTEXT(X)	1 (TRUE), if X is not text.
ISNUMBER(X)	1 (TRUE), if X contains a numeric value.
ISODD(X)	1 (TRUE), if the number is odd.
ISREF(X)	1 (TRUE), if X is a reference.

ISTEXT(X)	1 (TRUE), if X is text.
N(X)	A value converted to a number.
NA()	The error value #N/A.
TYPE(X)	A number indicating the data type value of X.

Logical Functions

Logical functions produce a value based on the result of a conditional statement, using numeric arguments. The various functions and what they return are as follows:

Function	*Returns*
AND(N1,N2,N3,..)	The logical value 1 (TRUE) if all its arguments are TRUE.
FALSE()	The logical value 0.
IF(Cr,X,Y)	The value X if Cr is TRUE and Y if Cr is FALSE.
IFERROR(Expres,Num)	The value Num if the Expres is in error.
NOT(N)	The reverse logic of its argument N.
OR(N1, N2, ..)	The logical value 1 (TRUE) if any argument is TRUE.
TRUE()	The logical value 1.

Lookup and Reference Functions

This group of functions return values specified by a range reference or array reference.

Function	*Return*s
ADDRESS(Rn,Cn)	The cell address specified by row Rn and column Cn.

AREAS(Rf1,Rf2,..)	The number of areas in the list of references.
CHOOSE(K,V0,..,Vn)	The Kth value in the list V0,..,Vn.
COLUMN(Rf)	The column number of a reference.
COLUMNS(Rg)	The number of columns in the range Rg.

GETPIVOTDATA(Df,Pt,Fd1,Im,Fd2,Im2,...)

The data stored in a PivotTable report. Df is the name (enclosed in quotation marks) for the data field that contains the data you want to retrieve, Pt is a reference to any cell, range of cells, or named range of cells in a PivotTable report, while Fd1, Im1, Fd2, Im2 are 1 to 126 pairs of field names and item names that describe the data you want to retrieve.

HLOOKUP(X,Ar,Rn)	The value of indicated cell by performing a horizontal array lookup by comparing the value X to each cell in the top index row in array Ar, then moves down the column in which a match is found by the specified row number Rn.
HYPERLINK(Loc,Fn)	A shortcut that opens a document stored on your hard disc, network server, or on the Internet.
INDEX(Rg,Rn,Cn)	The value of the cell in range Rg at the intersection of row-offset Rn, and column-offset Cn.

INDIRECT(Rf)	The cell reference specified in reference Rf in A1-style.
LOOKUP(Lv,Vr,Rv)	The relative position of an item in an array that matches a specified value in a specified order.
MATCH(Lv,Ar,Mtc)	The relative position of an element in an array Ar that matches the specified value Mtc of a lookup value Lv.
OFFSET(Rf,Rn,C,Ht,Wh)	A reference of a specified height Ht and width Wh offset from another reference Rf by a specified number of rows Rn and columns Cn.
ROW(Rf)	The row number of a reference.
ROWS(Rg)	The number of rows in a range.
RTD(Pid,Sr,Tc)	Real-time data from a program that supports COM automation, where Pid is id of a registered COM automation add-in program, Sr the server name where it is to be found, and Tc the data topic to be retrieved.
TRANSPOSE(Ar)	The transpose of an array.
VLOOKUP(X,Ar,Cn)	The value of indicated cell by performing a vertical table lookup by comparing the value X to each cell in the first index column, in array Ar, then moves across the row in which a match is found by the specified column number Cn.

Math and Trigonometry Functions

These functions evaluate a result using numeric arguments. The various functions and what they return are as follows:

Function	*Returns*
ABS(X)	The absolute value of X.
ACOS(X)	The angle in radians, whose cosine is X (arc cos of X).
ACOSH(N)	The arc (inverse) hyperbolic cosine of number N.
ASIN(X)	The angle in radians, whose sine is X (arc sin of X).
ASINH(N)	The arc (inverse) hyperbolic sine of number N.
ATAN(X)	The angle in radians, between $\pi/2$ and $-\pi/2$, whose tangent is X (arc tan of X - 2 quadrant).
ATAN2(X,Y)	The angle in radians, between π and $-\pi$, whose tangent is Y/X (arc tan of Y/X - 4 quadrant).
ATANH(N)	The arc (inverse) hyperbolic tangent of number N.
CEILING(N,Sig)	The rounded value of N to nearest integer or nearest multiple of significance Sig.
COMBIN(N,Obj)	The number of combinations N for a given number of objects Obj.
COS(X)	The cosine of X (X in radians).
COSH(X)	The hyperbolic cosine of X.
COUNTIF(Rg, Cr)	The number of non-blank cells within a range Rg.

DEGREES(X)	The value in degrees of X radians.
EVEN(X)	The rounded value of X away from 0 to the nearest even integer.
EXP(X)	The value of e raised to the power of X.
FACT(X)	The factorial of X.
FACTDOUBLE(X)	The double factorial of X.
FLOOR(N, Sig)	A number N rounded down towards zero by nearest multiple of significance Sig.
GCD(N1,N2,..)	The greatest common divisor of two or more integers.
INT(X)	The integer part of X.
LCM(N1,N2,...)	The least common multiple of two or more integers.
LN(X)	The natural log (base e) of X.
LOG(X,N)	The log of X to a specified base N.
LOG10(X)	The log (base 10) of X.
MDETERM(Ar)	The matrix determinant of an array.
MINVERSE(Ar)	The matrix inverse of an array.
MMULT(Ar1,Ar2)	The matrix product of two arrays.
MOD(X,Y)	The remainder of X/Y.
MROUND(N,M)	A number N rounded to the desired multiple M.
MULTINOMINAL(N1,N2,...)	The ratio of the factorial of a sum of values to the product of the factorials.

ODD(X)	The rounded value of X away from 0 to the nearest odd integer.
PI()	The value of π (3.1415926).
POWER(X,N)	The value of X raised to the power of N.
PRODUCT(Ls)	The result of multiplying the values in list Ls.
QUOTIENT(Nm,Dm)	The integer portion of a division, where Nm is the numerator, and Dm the denominator.
RADIANS(X)	The value in rads of X degrees.
RAND()	A random number between 0-1.
RANDBETWEEN(Bm,Tp)	A random number between the numbers bottom (Bm) and top (Tp) you specify.
ROMAN(N,Fm)	The Roman format Fm (as text) of number N.
ROUND(X,N)	The value of X rounded to N places.
ROUNDDOWN(X,N)	The rounded value of X down to the nearest multiple of the power of 10 specified by N.
ROUNDUP(X,N)	The rounded value of X up to the nearest multiple of the power of 10 specified by N.
SERIESSUM(X,N,M,Cs)	The sum of a power series based on a formula, where X is the input value of the power series, N the initial power to raise X, M the step increment of N for each term of the series, and Cs the set of coefficients by which each successive power of X is multiplied.

SIGN(X)	The value of 1 if X is a positive, 0 if X is 0, and −1 if X is negative.
SIN(X)	The sine of angle X (X in rads).
SINH(X)	The hyperbolic sine of angle X (X in rads).
SQRT(X)	The square root of X.
SQRTPI	Returns the square root of (number * pi).
SUBTOTAL(Ls)	The subtotal in a list Ls or a database.
SUM(Rg)	The sum of values in range Rg.
SUMIF(Rg,Cr)	The sum in range Rg that meet a given criteria Cr.
SUMPRODUCT(Ar1,Ar2)	The sum of the products of array components.
SUMSQ(N1,N2)	The sum of the squares of the arguments.
SUMX2MY2(Ar1,Ar2)	The sum of the difference of squares of corresponding values in two arrays.
SUMX2PY2(Ar1,Ar2)	The sum of the sum of squares of corresponding values in two arrays.
SUMXMY2(Ar1,Ar2)	The sum of squares of differences of corresponding values in two arrays.
TAN(X)	The tangent of angle X (X in rads).
TANH(X)	The hyperbolic tangent of angle X (X in rads).
TRUNC(X,N)	The truncated value of X to N decimal places.

Statistical Functions

Statistical functions evaluate lists of values using numeric arguments or cell ranges. The various functions and what they return are as follows:

Function	*Returns*
AVEDEV(Ls)	The average of the absolute deviations of values in list Ls.
AVERAGE(Rg)	The average of values in range Rg - text entries are ignored.
AVERAGEA(Rg)	The average (arithmetic mean) of values in range Rg, including logical values and text - logical TRUE evaluates as 1, while FALSE evaluates as 0.
AVERAGEIF(Rg,Cr)	The average (arithmetic mean) of all the cells in a range Rg that meet the criteria Cr.
AVERAGEIFS(Rg,Cr1,Cr2)	The average (arithmetic mean) of all the cells in a range Rg that meet multiple criteria Cr1, Cr2, etc.
BETADIST(X,Al,Bt,A,B)	The cumulative beta probability density function.
BETAINV(Pb,Al,Bt,A,B)	The inverse of the cumulative beta probability function.
BINOMDIST(Sc,Tr,Pb,Tp)	The cumulative distribution function if Tp is TRUE, else the probability mass function, with Tr independent trials and Sc successes in trials and Pr probability of success per trial.
CHIDIST(X,Fr)	The chi-square distribution, evaluated at X and Fr degrees of freedom for the sample.

CHINV(X,Fr)	The inverse of the one-tailed probability of the chi-squared distribution.
CHITEST(Rg1,Rg2)	The chi-square test for independence on the data in range Rg1, or a chi-square test for goodness of fit on the data in ranges Rg1 and Rg2.
CONFIDENCE(Al,Sd,Sz)	The confidence interval for a population mean.
COUNTBLANK(Rg)	The number of cells that are blank in a range Rg.
COUNTIF(Rg,Cr)	The number of cells within a range Rg that meet the criteria Cr.
COUNTIFS(Rg,Cr1,Cr2)	The number of cells within a range Rg that meet multiple criteria Cr1, Cr2, etc.
CORREL(Rg1,Rg2)	The correlation coefficient of values in ranges Rg1 and Rg2.
COUNT(Ls)	The number of values in a list.
COUNTA(Rg)	The number of non-blank values in a range Rg.
COVAR(Rg1,Rg2)	The sample covariance of the values in ranges Rg1 and Rg2.
CRITBINOM(Tr,Pb,Al)	The largest integer for which the cumulative binomial distribution is less than or equal to Al, with Tr Bernoulli trials and a probability of success for a single Bernoulli trial Pb.
DEVSQ(Ls)	The sum of squared deviations of the values in list Ls, from their mean.
EXPONDIST(X,Lm,Ds)	The exponential distribution.

FDIST(X,Fr1,Fr2)	The F-distribution at value X with Fr1 and Fr2 degrees of freedom for the first and second samples.
FINV(Pb,Fr1,Fr2)	The inverse of the F probability distribution.
FISHER(X)	The Fisher transformation.
FISHERINV(Y)	The inverse of the Fisher transformation.
FORECAST(X,Yo,Xo)	The value along a linear trend.
FREQUENCY(Rg,Bin)	The frequency distribution as a vertical array Bin.
FTEST(Rg1,Rg2)	The associated probability of an F-test on data in ranges Rg1 and Rg2. Used to determine if two samples have different variances.
GAMMADIST(X,Al,Bt,Cm)	The gamma distribution.
GAMMAINV(Pb,Al,Bt)	The inverse of the gamma cumulative distribution.
GAMMALN(X)	The natural logarithm of the gamma function.
GEOMEAN(Ls)	Returns the geometric mean of the values in list Ls.
GROWTH(Yo,Xo,Xn,Ct)	The values along an exponential trend.
HARMEAN(Ls)	The harmonic mean of the values in list Ls.
HYPGEOMDIST(Ns,Ssiz,Pp,Psiz)	
	The hypergeometric distribution probability of a given number of successes Ns, given the sample size Ssiz, population success Pp and population size Psiz.

INTERCEPT(Yo,Xo)	The intercept of the linear regression line.
KURT(Rg)	The kurtosis of the values in range Rg.
LARGE(Arr,K)	The largest value in a data set.
LINEST(Yo,Xo,Ct,St)	The parameters of a linear trend.
LOGEST(Yo,Xo,Ct,St)	The parameters of an exponential trend.
LOGINV(Pb,Mn,Sd)	The inverse of the lognormal distribution with parameters mean Mn and standard deviation Sd.

LOGNORMDIST(X,Mn,Sd)

The cumulative lognormal distribution with parameters mean Mn and standard deviation Sd.

MAX(Rg)	The maximum value in a range.
MAXA(Rg)	The maximum value in a range. Does not ignore logical values or text.
MEDIAN(Ls)	The median value in list Ls.
MIN(Rg)	The minimum value in a range.
MINA(Rg)	The minimum value in a range. Does not ignore logical values or text.
MODE(Ls)	The most common value in a data set.

NEGBINOMDIST(Nf,Ns,Pb)

The negative binomial distribution that there will be a number of failures Nf before the number of successes Ns, when the constant probability of success is Pb.

NORMDIST(X,Mn,Sd)	The normal cumulative distribution function for X, with a distribution mean Mn and optional standard deviation Sd.
NORMINV(Pb,Mn,Sd)	The inverse of the normal cumulative distribution.
NORMSDIST(X)	The standard normal cumulative distribution.
NORMSINV(Pb)	The inverse of the standard normal cumulative distribution.
PEARSON(Ar1,Ar2)	The Pearson product moment correlation coefficient.
PERCENTILE(Rg,K)	The Kth sample percentile among the values in range Rg.
PERCENTRANK(Ar,X,Sg)	The percentage rank of a value in a data set.
PERMUT(N,Nc)	The number of ordered sequences (permutations) of Nc chosen objects that can be selected from a total of N objects.
POISSON(X,Mn,Cm)	The Poisson distribution (depending on cumulative factor Cm) of X observed events and Mn expected number of events.
PROB(Rgx,Pb,Ll,Ul)	The probability that values in Rgx range are within lower limit Ll and upper limit Ul of probability Pb.
QUARTILE(Ar,Qrt)	The quartile of a data set.
RANK(It,Rg,Od)	The relative size or position of a value It in a range Rg, relative to other values in the range, ranked in order Od.
RSQ(Yo,Xo)	The square of the Pearson product moment correlation coefficient.

SKEW(Rg)	The skewness of the values in range Rg.
SLOPE(Yo,Xo)	The slope of the linear regression line.
SMALL(Ar,K)	The Kth smallest value in a data set.
STANDARDIZE(X,Mn,Sd)	The normalised value of X from a distribution characterised by mean Mn and standard deviation Sd.
STDEV(Rg)	The population standard deviation of values in range Rg.
STDEVA(Rg)	An estimate of the standard deviation based on a sample, including logical values and text.
STDEVP(Rg)	The standard deviation based on the entire population.
STDEVPA(Rg)	The standard deviation based on the entire population, including logical values and text.
STEYX(Yo,Xo)	The standard error of the predicted y-value for each X in the regression.
TDIST(X,Fr,Tr)	The Student's t-distribution, evaluated at X and Fr degrees of freedom for the sample, with test direction Tr.
TINV(Pb,Fr)	The inverse of the Student's t-distribution.
TREND(Xo,Yo,Xn,Cn)	The values along a linear trend.
TRIMMEAN(Ar,Pb)	The mean of the interior of a data set.
TTEST(Rg1,Rg2,Tl,Tp)	The probability associated with a Student's t-test.

VAR(Rg)	The sample variance of values in range Rg.
VARA(Rg)	An estimate of the variance based on a sample, including logical values and text.
VARP(Rg)	The variance of values in range Rg based on entire population.
VARPA(Rg)	The variance of values in range Rg based on entire population, including logical values and text.
WEIBULL(X,Al,Bt,Cm)	The Weibull distribution.
ZTEST(Arr,X,Sg)	The two-tailed P-value of a z-test.

Text Functions

Text functions operate on strings and produce numeric or string values dependent on the function.

Function	*Returns*
BAHTTEXT(N)	A text in Thai using the ß (baht) number format of the supplied number Nr.
CHAR(X)	The character that corresponds to the code number X.
CLEAN(Sg)	The specified string Sg having removed all non-printable characters from it.
CODE(Sg)	The code number for the first character in string Sg.
CONCATENATE(Sg1,Sg2)	
	One string made up of several strings.
DOLLAR(N,Dm)	A number in text form, using currency format.

EXACT(Sg1,Sg2)	The value 1 (TRUE) if strings Sg1 and Sg2 are exactly alike, otherwise 0 (FALSE).
FIND(Ss,Sg,Sn)	The position at which the first occurrence of search string Ss begins in string Sg, starting the search from search number Sn.
FIXED(N,Dm,Nc)	A number N formatted as text with a fixed number of decimals Dm. If Nc is 1 (TRUE) it prevents the inclusion of commas.
LEFT(Sg,N)	The first (leftmost) N characters in string Sg.
LEN(Sg)	The number of characters in string Sg.
LOWER(Sg)	A string Sg with all the letters converted to lowercase.
MID(Sg,Sn,N)	The N characters from string Sg beginning with the character at Sn.
PROPER(Sg)	A string with all words in string Sg changed to first letter in uppercase and the rest in lowercase.
REPLACE(O,S,N,Ns)	A string with N characters removed from original string O, starting at character S and then inserts new string Ns in the vacated place.
REPT(Sg,N)	A repeated string Sg, N times. Unlike the repeating character (\), the output is not limited by the column width.
RIGHT(Sg,N)	The last (rightmost) N characters in string Sg.

SEARCH(Sg1,O,S)	String Sg1 in original string O, starting at character S.
SUBSTITUTE(Sg,O,Ns,N)	A new string Ns substituted for old string O in a string Sg. N specifies which occurrence of the old text you want to replace.
T(X)	A value X converted into text.
TEXT(X,Fm)	A number X formatted into text.
TRIM(Sg)	A string Sg with no leading, trailing or consecutive spaces.
UPPER(Sg)	All letters in string Sg converted to uppercase.
VALUE(Sg)	The numeric value of string Sg.

13

Glossary of Terms

Add-in	A mini-program which runs in conjunction with another and enhances its functionality.
Address	A unique number or name that identifies a specific computer or user on a network.
Anonymous FTP	Anonymous FTP allows you to connect to a remote computer and transfer public files back to your computer without the need for a user ID and password.
Application	Software (program) designed to carry out certain activity, such as word processing, or data management.
Archiving	A way of storing old e-mail messages in a compacted form.
Association	An identification of a file name extension to a program. This lets Windows open the program when its files are selected.
Attachment	A file that is added to an e-mail message for transmission.
Backup	To make a back-up copy of a file or a disc for safekeeping.

Bitmap | A technique for managing the image displayed on a computer screen.

Bookmark | A marker inserted at a specific point in a document. Used as a target for a hypertext link, or to enable a user to return for later reference.

Browse | A button in some Windows dialogue boxes that lets you view a list of files and folders before you make a selection.

Browser | A program, like the Internet Explorer, that lets you view Web pages.

Bug | An error in coding or logic that causes a program to malfunction.

Button | A graphic element in a dialogue box or toolbar that performs a specified function.

CD-ROM | Compact Disc – Read Only Memory; an optical disc from which information may be read but not written to.

Chart | A graphical view of data that is used to visually display trends, patterns, and comparisons.

Client | A computer that has access to services over a computer network. The computer providing the services is a server.

Client application	A Windows application that can accept linked or embedded objects.
Clipboard	A temporary storage area of memory, where text and graphics are stored with the Windows cut and copy actions.
Command	An instruction given to a computer to carry out a particular action.
Compressed file	One that is compacted to save server space and reduce transfer times. Typical file extensions for compressed files include .zip (DOS/Windows) and .tar (UNIX).
Configuration	A general term referring to the way you have your computer set up.
Context menu	A menu that opens when you right-click the mouse button on a feature.
CPU	The Central Processing Unit; the main chip that executes all instructions entered into a computer.
Database	A collection of data related to a particular topic or purpose.
DBMS	Database management system – a software interface between the database and the user.
Dial-up Connection	A popular form of Net connection for the home user, over standard telephone lines.

Default	The command, device or option automatically chosen.
Desktop	The Windows screen working background, on which you place icons, folders, etc.
Device driver	A special file that must be loaded into memory for Windows to be able to address a specific procedure or hardware device.
Device name	A logical name used by DOS and Windows to identify a device, such as LPT1 or COM1 for the parallel or serial printer.
Dialogue box	A window displayed on the screen to allow the user to enter information.
Directory	An area on disc where information relating to a group of files is kept. Also known as a folder.
Disc	A device on which you can store programs and data.
Document	A file produced by an application program.
Domain	A group of devices, servers and computers on a network.
Domain Name	The name of an Internet site, for example www.microsoft.com, which allows you to reference Internet sites without knowing their true numerical address.
Download	To transfer to your computer a file, or data, from another computer.

DPI	Dots Per Inch – a resolution standard for laser printers.
Drag	To move an object on the screen by pressing and holding down the left mouse button while moving the mouse.
Drive name	The letter followed by a colon which identifies a floppy or hard disc drive.
Drop-down list	A menu item that can be clicked to open extra items that can be selected.
Embedded object	Information in a document that is 'copied' from its source application. Selecting the object opens the creating application from within the document.
Engine	Software used by search services.
Encryption	A method of making data or e-mail messages private by converting them into a secure form which then needs a special key to unlock or decrypt it.
Ethernet	A very common method of networking computers in a LAN.
FAQ	Frequently Asked Questions – a common feature on the Internet, FAQs are files of answers to commonly asked questions.
File extension	The suffix following the period in a filename. Windows uses this to identify the source application

	program. For example .xls indicates an Excel file.
Filename	The name given to a file. In Windows 95/98 and above this can be up to 256 characters long.
Filter	A set of criteria that is applied to data to show a subset of the data.
Folder	An area used to store a group of files, usually with a common link.
Font	A graphic design representing a set of characters, numbers and symbols.
FTP	File Transfer Protocol. The procedure for connecting to a remote computer and transferring files.
Function key	One of the series of 10 or 12 keys marked with the letter F and a numeral, used for specific operations.
GIF	Graphics Interchange Format, a common standard for images on the Web.
Graphic	A picture or illustration, also called an image. Formats include GIF, JPEG, BMP, PCX, and TIFF.
Graphics card	A device that controls the display on the monitor and other allied functions.
GUI	A Graphic User Interface, such as Windows, the software front-end

	that provides an easy to use interface.
Hard copy	Output on paper.
Hard disc	A device built into the computer for holding programs and data.
Hardware	The equipment that makes up a computer system, excluding the programs or software.
Help	A Windows system that gives you instructions and additional information on using a program.
Home page	The document displayed when you first open your Web browser, or the first document you come to at a Web site.
Host	Computer connected directly to the Internet that provides services to other local and/or remote computers.
HTML	HyperText Markup Language, the format used in documents on the Web.
HTML editor	Authoring tool which assists with the creation of HTML pages.
HTTP	HyperText Transport Protocol, the system used to link and transfer hypertext documents on the Web.
Hyperlink	A segment of text, or an image, that refers to another document on the Web, an Intranet or your PC.

Hypermedia	Hypertext extended to include linked multimedia.
Hypertext	A system that allows documents to be cross-linked so that the reader can explore related links, or documents, by clicking on a highlighted symbol.
Icon	A small graphic image that represents a function or object. Clicking on an icon produces an action.
Image	See 'Graphic'.
IMAP	Internet message access protocol – used for the transfer of Web pages and Web mail.
Insertion point	A flashing bar that shows where typed text will be entered into a document.
Interface	A device that allows you to connect a computer to its peripherals.
Internet	The global system of computer networks.
Intranet	A private network inside an organisation using the same kind of software as the Internet.
IP	Internet Protocol – the rules that provide basic Internet functions.
IP Address	Internet Protocol Address – every computer on the Internet has a unique identifying number.
ISDN	Integrated Services Digital Network, a telecom standard using

digital transmission technology to support voice, video and data communications applications over regular telephone lines.

ISP

Internet Service Provider – a company that offers access to the Internet.

Java

An object-oriented programming language created by Sun Microsystems for developing applications and applets that are capable of running on any computer, regardless of the operating system.

JPEG/JPG

Joint Photographic Experts Group, a popular cross-platform format for image files. JPEG is best suited for true colour original images.

Keyword

A word used by a database application or Office's Clip Art to locate specific information or images.

Kilobyte

(KB); 1024 bytes of information or storage space.

LAN

Local Area Network – high-speed, privately-owned network covering a limited geographical area, such as an office or a building.

Laptop

A portable computer small enough to sit on your lap.

LCD

Liquid Crystal Display.

Links	The hypertext connections between Web pages.
Local	A resource that is located on your computer, not linked to it over a network.
Location	An Internet address.
Log on	To gain access to a network.
Mail Merge	The ability to send the same letter to any number of people, but personalise it by inserting their own name and address – usually held in a database.
MAPI	Messaging application programming interface – a messaging architecture and client side interface for applications such as e-mail.
MCI	Media Control Interface – a standard for files and multimedia devices.
Megabyte	(MB); 1024 kilobytes of information or storage space.
Megahertz	(MHz); Speed of processor in millions of cycles per second.
Memory	Part of computer consisting of storage elements organised into addressable locations that can hold data and instructions.
Menu	A list of available options in an application.

Menu bar	The horizontal bar that lists the names of menus.
MIDI	Musical Instrument Digital Interface – enables devices to transmit and receive sound and music messages.
MIME	Multipurpose Internet Mail Extensions, a messaging standard that allows Internet users to exchange e-mail messages enhanced with graphics, video and voice.
Modem	Short for modulator-demodulator devices. An electronic device that lets PCs communicate electronically.
Monitor	The display device connected to your PC, also called a screen.
Mouse	A device used to manipulate a pointer around your display and activate processes by pressing buttons.
MPEG	Motion Picture Experts Group – a video file format offering excellent quality in a relatively small file.
Multimedia	The use of photographs, music and sound and movie images in a presentation.
Network	Two or more computers connected together to share resources.
Network server	Central computer which stores files for several linked computers.

OLE	Object Linking and Embedding – a technology for transferring and sharing information among software applications.
Online	Having access to the Internet.
Operating system	Software that runs a computer.
Page	An HTML document, or Web site.
Paragraph Style	Includes font, size, alignment, line spacing, indents, style and other formatting options.
Password	A unique character string used to gain access to a network or program.
PATH	The location of a file in the directory tree.
Peripheral	Any device attached to a PC.
Pixel	A picture element on screen; the smallest element that can be independently assigned colour and intensity.
Plug-and-play	Hardware which can be plugged into a PC and be used immediately without configuration.
POP3	Post Office Protocol – a method of storing and returning e-mail.
Print queue	A list of print jobs waiting to be sent to a printer.
Program	A set of instructions which cause a computer to perform tasks.

Protocol	A set of rules or standards that defines how computers communicate with each other.
Query	The set of keywords and operators sent by a user to a search engine, or a database search request.
RAM	Random Access Memory. The computer's volatile memory. Data held in it is lost when power is switched off.
Resource	See 'Shared resource'.
ROM	Read Only Memory. A PC's non-volatile memory. Data is written into this memory at manufacture and is not affected by power loss.
RTF	Rich Text Format. An enhanced form of text that includes basic formatting and is used for transferring data between applications, or in e-mail messages.
Scroll bar	A bar that appears at the right side or bottom edge of a window.
Search	Submit a query to a search engine.
Search engine	A program that helps users find information across the Internet.
Server	A computer system that manages and delivers information for client computers.
Shared resource	Any device, program or file that is available to network users.

Signature file	An ASCII text file, maintained within e-mail programs, that contains text for your signature.
Site	A place on the Internet. Every Web page has a location where it resides which is called its site.
Smart Tag	A button that, when clicked, opens a shortcut menu to give fast access to other features or Office applications.
Software	The programs and instructions that control your PC.
Spooler	Software which handles transfer of information to a store to be used by a peripheral device.
SVGA	Super Video Graphics Array; it has all the VGA modes but with 256, or more, colours.
Swap file	An area of your hard disc used to store temporary operating files, also known as virtual memory.
System disc	A disc containing files to enable a PC to start up.
Task bar	The bar that by default is located at the bottom of your screen whenever Windows is running. It contains the Start button, buttons for all the applications that are open, and icons for other applications.

Task Pane | A pane or sub-window that gives a range of options pertaining to the task currently being performed.

TCP/IPTransmission | Control Protocol/ Internet Protocol, combined protocols that perform the transfer of data between two computers. TCP monitors and ensures the correct transfer of data. IP receives the data, breaks it up into packets, and sends it to a network within the Internet.

Text file | An unformatted file of text characters saved in ASCII format.

Thumbnail | A small graphic image.

TIFF | Tagged-Image File Format – a popular graphic image file format.

Toolbar | A bar containing icons giving quick access to commands.

Toggle | To turn an action on and off with the same switch.

TrueType fonts | Fonts that can be scaled to any size and print as they show on the screen.

Upload/Download | The process of transferring files between computers. Files are uploaded from your computer to another and downloaded from another computer to your own.

URL | Uniform Resource Locator, the addressing system used on the Web.

User ID	The unique identifier, usually used in conjunction with a password, which identifies you on a computer.
Virus	A malicious program, downloaded from a web site or disc, designed to wipe out information on your computer.
WAV	Waveform Audio (.wav) – a common audio file format used by computers.
Web	A network of hypertext-based multimedia information servers.
Web Page	An HTML document that is accessible on the Web.
Web Queries	A way to get data from a Web page into Excel so that you can work with it.
WINSOCK	A Microsoft Windows file that provides the interface to TCP/IP services.
Wizard	A Microsoft tool that asks you questions and then creates an object depending on your answers.
XML	Extensible markup language – allows you to use tags to specify the structure of data. Excel worksheet data saved in XML format can be used by other applications.

Index